Tortillas Wraps & Co.

Exquisitely Filled Dishes

© Naumann & Göbel Verlagsgesellschaft mbH, a subsidiary of
VEMAG Verlags- und Medien Aktiengesellschaft, Cologne
www.apollo-intermedia.de

Translation: Maureen Millington-Brodie
Complete production: Naumann & Göbel Verlagsgesellschaft mbH, Cologne
Printed in Italy

ISBN 3-625-11126-8

Tortillas Wraps & Co.

Exquisitely Filled Dishes

NAUMANN & GÖBEL

Contents

Exquisitely Filled and Deliciously Wrapped

Nearly all cuisines in the world know them:
the small appetising pockets, mini rolls or little
parcels with their exciting fillings. A culinary experience
in ever new delicious variations – we hereby invite
you to try the entire spectrum of wrapped delicacies!
Whether ravioli with fine mushroom filling, small spicy
strudels, crispy spring rolls or hearty filled wraps – the
beloved snacks from America: our recipe ideas
are simple to prepare whatever the case!

A Culinary Round the World Trip

The history of the small cute parcels, bites, mini rolls and pockets is at one and the same time a culinary trip around the world. We would like to introduce you in advance to the classics amongst the international "packaged specialities" which you will of course find in clever variations in this book as well. Do also try our original new recipe suggestions which will present you with the entire colourful palette of wrapping and filling possibilities – with vegetables or fruit, meat or fish, savoury or sweet!

Spring Rolls

The idea of serving a meal in bites or in "compact" form is nothing new. Asian cuisine has, for instance, been acquainted with this technique for more than a thousand years. Thus filled and crispy fried or baked rolls made from a type of pancake batter are a traditional speciality for the Chinese New Year festivities in China. As this simultaneously also celebrates the end of the dark days of winter and the start of the coming spring, these rolls are also called "spring rolls" – and, under this appellation, enjoy great popularity the world over. Their fillings are enormously varied. You can find frozen or dried spring roll casings in specialist grocery shops or in Asian supermarkets which you can then fill as you like and prepare very simply!

Wan-Tans

Another Asian classic are small purses or pockets made out of a kind of noodle dough. Depending on the region they are called, for example, wan-tans, dim sums or sui-mais. The same thing is meant by all these: exquisite filled dough casings in original shapes which are steamed, fried or baked.

Sushis

In the meantime now also thoroughly popular in Britain is sushi, a Japanese speciality in countless shapes, colours and variations. These artistically shaped, rolled or pressed bites made from cooked rice, raw fish and other ingredients such as vegetables – mostly wrapped or held together by Nori leaves and wasabi paste – are a demonstration of Japanese food culture of the most refined kind. The origin of sushis is quite practical: presumably rice pickled with vinegar served in days gone by to preserve raw fish and seafood; the rice itself was therefore not eaten with them in those days. Over the course of time, an individual food culture developed out of this which is cultivated and tended in Japan with much love.

Amongst the most well-known sushi variations are:

Maki-Sushis
These are rolled sushi in various sizes and combinations. Nori leaves are used in making these and are spread with rice, which is coloured or white according to desire, then filled with ingredients and rolled up with the help of a bamboo mat. Then the rolls are cut into handy pieces.

Temaki-Sushis
With these the rice is rolled up with the ingredients in a thin sheet (of lettuce, vegetable, omelette or similar) into small cones.

Gunkan-Maki-Sushis
These have the shape of small boats which consist of a Nori leaf and rice filling upon which the rest of the ingredients are distributed as desired.

Let us leave the cuisine of Asia and turn to another part of the Earth which has in no lesser way also cultivated the cuisine of filled dishes and exported them to the entire world: Central and South America. In cleverness and taste they stand equal with the Asian delicacies and are almost as well-known as pizza in the British kitchen.

Tortillas
The thin maize or wheat flatbreads of Mexican cuisine are in the meantime just as popular as the American sandwich. They are more or less the bread of Mexican cuisine and are put out as accompaniment to nearly all dishes. We know them mainly rolled up or folded together with splendid fillings of vegetables and meat.

Burritos
These are tortillas with a meat filling which are folded over on one side and then rolled up. The other, open, side allows an appetizing view of the filling.

Flautas
This is what Tortilla rolls are called which are long, thin and open on both sides. Before serving they are browned quickly in the frying pan on all sides. They are called this because of their flute-like shape ("flauta" being the Spanish word for flute).

Enchiladas
This name disguises tortillas which are served with chilli sauce or which have been baked with a cheese covering.

Wraps
They are also winning over many fans here too: American wraps – a kind of combination of burritos and classic sandwiches. The tortilla flatbreads can be filled differently again and again according to taste and can be served open or closed.

Tacos
These are tortillas which have been shaped into dishes and which can be filled differently again and again according to choice and imagination. They are now available in any well-stocked supermarket as a ready-made product.

Quesadillas
This type of cake consists of tortillas layered with a filling. Before serving they are cut into triangles.

Tamales
For these a soft maize flour dough is spread onto dried maize leaves and then steamed in them. In the majority of cases the dough is then filled.

Around the Mediterranean too people like tasty food inside handy packets. You can find filo or yufka pastry sheets with sweet to hot spicy fillings not only in Greek and Turkish but also in Arab cuisines not to mention the **pitas**, **flatbreads** or tasty **stuffed vine leaves** which have in the meanwhile moved across into central European cookery. In Southern Europe the filled delicacies are for instance called **empanadas** – pockets e.g. from puff pastry, which are cooked in oil or baked in the oven – or **ravioli**, Italian dough pockets out of wheat flour which these days you can find with countless variations in fillings from meat, vegetables and cream cheese.

In the Eastern European cuisines people love **piroggis** for example: triangular or crescent-shaped pastries made from yeast, puff pastry or short-crust pastry. In Russia, for example, "piraschki" are a national dish. These are piroggis with a hearty, very rich filling made out of meat, vegetables, pastes, herbs or even curd cheese, fruit and eggs.

Also the German kitchen is only too well acquainted with the phenomenon of encased titbits: Swabian **maultaschen**, the famous **windbeutel** or filled pancakes are just a few examples. We are also inordinately fond of **strudel** from Austria, paper-thin pastry with a very rich filling.

Great Britain too has its own special tradition of "food in an edible wrapping". From the ubiquitous **sausage roll**, long a favourite of the lunch box or party buffet, to the traditional lunch of the Cornish tin miner, the **Cornish pasty**. There are also the other meat favourites: **steak and kidney pies**, **Melton Mowbray pork pies** and **game pies**. Fruit pies, particular apple, are also a firm favourite. Every child remembers helping in the kitchen and making **jam tarts** out of left-over pastry. Nor would Christmas be complete without **mince pies**.

Has this overview – of course, very incomplete – woken your appetite? Then let us entice you with our delicious recipe ideas which present to you the classics of the packet cuisine in new and enhanced variations whilst leaving you much room to manoeuvre for your own ideas and creativity in the kitchen. In addition, in the following chapters you will find original creations which invite you to try them out and eat like a king. Whether rolled or folded, clapped together or twisted – enjoy the splendidly encased and cleverly filled treats!

Deliciously Packed: Vegetarian Dishes

Discover vegetables and grains afresh: as ideal ingredients for fillings, which are quick to cook, versatile to combine and, on top of all this, so downright delicious! Not only fine grains can be used effortlessly for these. Vegetables too can be cut up finely for every kind of casing without problem. There are no more obstacles to a hearty and healthy enjoyment!

Asian Noodle Purses

Preparation Time: approx. 1 hour

512 kcal/2152 kJ

Serves 4

250 g/9 oz plain wholemeal flour
100 g/3 ½ oz plain flour
2 eggs
salt
1 pinch ground coriander
1 pinch ground cardamom
250 ml/9 fl oz sparkling water
1 piece of fresh ginger (1 cm/½ in)
½ bunch of spring onions
100 g/3 ½ oz of tinned bamboo shoots
1 red pepper
2 stalks of celery
150 g/5 oz of tinned straw mushrooms
pepper
powdered mustard
3 Tbsp chilli oil
600 ml/1 pint 1 fl oz Asian stock
hoisin sauce for serving

1 Knead the flour together with the eggs, spices and sparkling water into a workable dough, allow to stand for 15 minutes. Peel and grate the ginger.

2 Clean and wash the spring onions and cut into rings. Drain the bamboo shoots and cut into pieces. Wash the red pepper, cut in half, core and cut into small dice.

3 Clean and wash the celery and cut into pieces. Drain the straw mushrooms in a sieve.

4 Shape the noodle dough into a roll and cut into 12 pieces. Then roll out the pieces of dough on a floured work surface into thin circles with a diameter of about 12 cm/3 in.

5 Place a portion of the filling onto the middle of each circle and season with salt, pepper and powdered mustard. Then drizzle oil onto each. Brush the edges of the dough with water and twist them into little purses.

6 Steam in the steamer or in a bamboo basket over the Asian stock for about 12 minutes. Arrange the purses on plates and serve with hoisin sauce.

> ### TIP
> *The Asian noodle purses are very suitable as party food. They are really good to prepare in advance and should be steamed lightly once again shortly before serving.*

Rice and Vegetable Quesadillas

Preparation Time: approx. 35 minutes

1025 kcal/4305 kJ

Serves 4

120 g/4 ¼ oz of wild rice
375 ml/13 fl oz vegetable stock
salt
350 g/12 oz mozzarella
1 bunch of coriander
5 Tbsp hot salsa
3 ready-made tortillas
350 g/12 oz frozen farmer's vegetables
400 ml/14 fl oz mushroom stock
100 g/3 ½ oz of grated Appenzell cheese
hot salsa for serving

1 Cook the rice according to the instructions on the packet in the vegetable stock with a bit of salt. Pre-heat the oven to 160 °C/ 320 °F/gas mark 2/3.

2 Drain the mozzarella and cut into thin strips. Wash the coriander, dry and chop finely.

3 Mix the mozzarella with coriander and salsa. Add the cooked rice. Bake the tortillas in the oven on the middle shelf for 5 minutes on each side.

4 Cook the farmer's vegetables for 4 minutes in the mushroom stock, then drain. Place one portion of rice and one portion of farmer's vegetables onto each tortilla.

5 Cover the whole with another tortilla and then with the remaining rice and vegetables, then sprinkle with cheese. Place the third tortilla on top and allow the cheese to melt in the oven.

6 Cut the double-decker into triangles and serve with some salsa.

TIP

If you can't get hold of any tortillas then use homemade pancakes, instead of Appenzell cheese you can also use a strong cheddar.

with Wasabi Paste

Preparation Time: approx. 20 minutes

164 kcal/688 kJ

Serves 4

3 Nori leaves
200 g/7 oz of red sushi rice cooked in beetroot juice
¼ tsp wasabi paste
200 g/7 oz of orange-coloured sushi rice cooked in pumpkin juice
1 bamboo mat for rolling up

1 Dry roast two Nori leaves on one side in a frying pan without fat and cut in half. Place a portion of red rice on each of the four pieces, spread with some wasabi paste and roll up with the help of the bamboo mat.

2 Press the rolls from the outside so that they are no longer round in cross-section but triangular.

3 Dry roast the third Nori leaf likewise on one side, lay flat and then spread with the orange-coloured rice. Coat with some wasabi paste.

4 Place the smaller four rolls onto the rice and roll up into one large roll. Cut the large roll up into four slices and serve.

Roll up the four rolls.

Give a triangular shape.

Place the four rolls onto the rice.

Roll them all up.

Hearty German Pasta Pockets

Preparation Time: approx. 45 minutes

992 kcal/4168 kJ

Serves 4

350 g/12 oz plain wholemeal flour
3 eggs, salt
1 tsp each of chopped oregano and basil
125 ml/4 ½ fl oz sparkling water
2 cl wheat beer
5 shallots
3 cloves of garlic
600 g/1 lb 5 oz of tinned tomatoes
150 g/5 oz pitted black olives
2 Tbsp capers
4 Tbsp olive oil
4 slices of pumpernickel
4 Tbsp of white breadcrumbs cayenne pepper
100 g/3 ½ oz of grated Appenzell cheese
100 g/3 ½ oz of roasted onion butter

1 Work the flour with the eggs, salt, chopped herbs, sparkling water and wheat beer into a workable dough. Allow to stand for 10 minutes. Peel the shallots and garlic and dice. Drain the tomatoes, olives and capers and cut into small pieces. Heat the oil in a frying pan. Cook the shallots lightly with the garlic, olives and capers. Add the tomatoes. Crumble the pumpernickel slices to crumbs and mix in with the white breadcrumbs. Season with salt and pepper. Stir the cheese into the mixture.

2 Roll out the dough on a floured surface and cut out circles. Place a portion of the filling onto each circle and fold shut. Press the edges together. Cook them in salted boiling water for 10 minutes. Finally take out. Heat the roasted onion butter and fry the pasta pockets for about 4 minutes. Serve immediately.

Fortune Rolls

Preparation Time: approx. 30 minutes

252 kcal/1060 kJ

Serves 4

16 sheets of rice paper
16 red oak leaf lettuce leaves
200 g/7 oz of rice noodles
500 ml/18 fl oz of miso stock
1 bunch of spring onions
500 g/1 lb 2 oz of bottled salsify
3 Tbsp fish sauce
3 Tbsp soy sauce
1 bunch of coriander
1 tsp wasabi paste
1 carton of mustard cress
plum sauce or sweet-and-sour sauce to serve

1 Lay the rice paper onto one hot damp tea towel and cover with a second one. Allow to imbue for about 15 minutes. Wash the lettuce leaves, dry and spread out onto a work surface.

2 Poor hot miso stock onto the rice noodles and allow to swell. Clean and wash the spring onions and cut into rings.

3 Pour the liquid off the salsify and allow to drain before slicing.

4 Drizzle the fish and soy sauce onto the salsify and spring onions.

5 Wash and dry the coriander, chop finely and add to the vegetables. Drain the noodles and cut into short lengths, then mix with the vegetables.

6 Thinly spread the rice paper with some wasabi paste and lay one lettuce leaf on each. Place a portion of the filling onto each leaf and fold the sides of the rice paper over it.

7 Roll up the whole ensemble. Cut the cress from the carton and wash, arrange the fortune rolls on top of it. Serve with plum or sweet-and-sour sauce.

Samosas

Preparation Time: approx. 1 hour and 20 minutes

852 kcal/3580 kJ

Serves 4

300 g/10 ½ oz plain wholemeal spelt flour

50 g/1 ¾ oz plain flour

250 ml/9 fl oz sparkling water

salt

ground coriander, cumin and cardamom

4 Tbsp walnut oil

400 g/14 oz bottled sweet potatoes

250 g/9 oz bottled pickled sweet and sour pumpkin

½ cucumber

1 bunch of spring onions

3 Tbsp sesame oil

2 Tbsp light soy sauce

cayenne

1 bunch of coriander

2 Tbsp of roasted sesame seeds

100 g/3 ½ oz of grated Gouda cheese

mango chutney to serve

Variation

Shape the pastry into small cones and modify the filling as follows: use tinned chickpeas instead of the pumpkin. Replace the spring onions with shallots, also dice and add 3 tomatoes.

1 Work the flour together with the sparkling water, salt, ground coriander, cumin and cardamom and oil into a smooth dough. Allow to rest for about 15 minutes.

2 In the meantime, pour the liquid off the sweet potatoes and pumpkin and allow to drain. Cut both into small pieces.

3 Wash the cucumber and dice. Clean and wash the spring onions and chop finely.

4 Heat the sesame oil in a frying pan and brown the sweet potato, pumpkin, cucumber and spring onions. Season to taste with the soy sauce, salt and cayenne.

5 Wash the coriander, dry it and then detach the leaves. Add them to the vegetables together with the sesame seeds. Heat the oven to 180 °C/355 °F/gas mark 4. Roll out the pastry on a floured surface and cut into 12 squares measuring about 10 x 10 cm/ 4 x 4 in.

6 Divide up the filling between the squares and place in such a way that the pastry can be folded in half diagonally to cover the filling. Lightly press the sides together. Sprinkle the cheese over the samosas. Line a baking sheet with baking paper and lay the samosas on it.

7 Bake them in the oven on the middle shelf for about 40 minutes. Turn the samosas over halfway through the baking time. Serve them warm with mango chutney.

Detach the coriander leaves.

Divide the filling.

Fold the pastry diagonally.

Lightly press the sides together.

Vegetable Tofu Rolls

Preparation Time: approx. 45 minutes

832 kcal/3496 kJ

Serves 4

16 sheets of frozen spring roll pastry
400 g/14 oz tofu
8 Tbsp soy sauce
8 Tbsp rice wine
2 Tbsp Chinese five spice
2 red peppers
200 g/7 oz mange tout
200 g/7 oz tinned sweet corn
1 onion, 2 cloves of garlic
100 g/3 ½ oz soya bean sprouts
1 piece of fresh ginger (3 cm/1 ¾ in)
4 Tbsp sesame oil, 1 Tbsp chilli oil
salt, pepper
oil for deep frying
lettuce leaves and chilli sauce for serving

1 Wrap up the sheets of dough in damp cloths and allow to defrost. In the meantime drain the tofu and cube.

2 Mix together the soy sauce, rice wine and Chinese five spice in a bowl. Drizzle the mixture over the tofu. Wash the peppers, cut into halves, core and dice finely.

3 Clean the mange tout, wash and cut into narrow strips. Drain the sweet corn.

4 Peel the onions and dice. Peel the garlic cloves and chop finely. Wash the bean sprouts and dry. Peel the ginger and grate.

5 Heat the oil in a frying pan and lightly cook the peppers, mange tout, sweet corn, onion, garlic and soya bean sprouts. Season with ginger, salt and pepper.

6 Spread out the sheets of pastry on a work surface and distribute the vegetables and the tofu cubes diagonally onto the pastry sheets (not quite to the edge).

7 Lay one part of the dough over the filling and fold both sides over this. Roll up the whole thing and dampen the edge with water and make fast.

8 Then deep fry the rolls in hot fat until golden brown. Arrange the rolls on lettuce leaves and serve with chilli sauce.

Stuffed Vine Leaves

Preparation Time: approx. 45 minutes

997 kcal/4189 kJ

Serves 4

3 Tbsp olive oil
150 g/5 oz bulgar wheat
1 l/1 ¾ pints vegetable stock
1 courgette, 2 onions
1 clove of garlic
100g/3 ½ oz of pitted black olives
2 Tbsp olive oil, salt, pepper
ground cumin and coriander
200 g/7 oz passata
16 pickled vine leaves
200 ml/7 fl oz white wine
herby mayonnaise dip to serve

1 Heat the oil in a frying pan and place the bulgar in it, turning until lightly cooked. Pour in half the stock and allow the bulgur to swell for about 10 minutes. Clean and wash the courgette and dice. Peel the onions and likewise dice. Peel the clove of garlic and chop finely. Drain the olives and cut into pieces.

2 Heat the oil in a frying pan and lightly cook the courgette, onions, garlic and olives in it. Season the mixture with salt, pepper, ground cumin and coriander. Add the passata. After about 4 minutes add the drained bulgar.

3 Drain the vine leaves and spread out onto a work surface. Place some filling onto each vine leaf, roll up and make fast, tucking the sides in as you do this. Heat the remaining stock and the wine in a large shallow pan and let the rolls simmer in this for about 5 minutes. Serve lukewarm with a herby mayonnaise dip.

INFO
The young leaves of the vine are served stuffed with mince, rice, mint and poultry, amongst other ingredients, mainly in the countries of the Eastern Mediterranean.

Fine Vegetable Tempura

Preparation Time: approx. 35 minutes

477 kcal/2005 kJ

Serves 4

250 g/9 oz of green asparagus
300 g/10 ½ oz of broccoli
300 g/10 ½ oz of cauliflower
750 ml/1 pint 7 fl oz of Asian stock
3 Tbsp apple vinegar
3 Tbsp dry sherry
3 Tbsp soy sauce
1 piece of fresh ginger (1 cm/½ in)
1 dried chilli
4 tomatoes
1 bunch of spring onions
1 bunch coriander
200 ml/7 fl oz sparkling water
200 ml/7 fl oz white wine
4 egg yolks
1 Tbsp dried lemongrass
250 g/9 oz plain flour
flour to dust
oil for deep frying

1 Clean and wash the asparagus, cut off the bottom ends. Clean and wash the cauliflower and divide into florets. Blanche everything in the stock for about 4 minutes.

2 Stir the vinegar with the sherry, soy sauce, grated ginger and crumbled chilli. Clean and wash the tomatoes, then dice.

3 Clean and wash the spring onions and cut into rings. Wash the coriander, dry and finely chop the leaves. Mix the sauce, tomatoes, spring onions and coriander together and allow to cool.

4 Stir the sparkling water and the white wine together. Beat the egg yolks and mix in. Mix in the lemongrass and flour and stir to obtain a smooth batter.

5 Pour the cooking liquid off the vegetables and allow to drain. Dust with flour and then dip into the batter.

6 Heat up the oil in a deep fat fryer or a pan and deep fry the vegetables in it until golden brown. Then place on kitchen towel to soak up the excess fat and serve with the tomato salsa.

Stir the batter's ingredients together.

Dust the vegetables with flour.

Dip everything into the batter.

Deep fry in hot oil.

Thai Spring Rolls

Preparation Time: approx. 50 minutes

279 kcal/1174 kJ

Serves 4

12 sheets of rice paper
200 g/7 oz of Chinese wheat noodles
1 l/1 ¾ pints of mushroom stock
3 Tbsp sesame oil
150 g/5 oz shiitake mushrooms
4 carrots
200 g/7 oz green beans
4 shallots
4 Tbsp groundnut oil
1 Tbsp chilli oil
2 cloves of garlic
1 piece of fresh ginger (3 cm/1 ¾ in)
1 red chilli
2 Tbsp fish sauce
2 Tbsp soy sauce
salt, pepper
1 Tbsp chopped lemongrass
oil for deep frying

1 Lay the rice paper out onto a damp tea towel, spray with water and cover with another damp tea towel. Prepare the noodles as per the instructions on the packet in the mushroom stock. Drain and cut into 2 cm/ 1 in long pieces. Mix with oil.

2 Wash the mushrooms and cut into pieces. Clean and wash the carrots and cut into batons. Clean and wash the beans and cut into pieces. Peel the shallots and dice finely. Heat the oil in a frying pan and lightly cook the mushrooms, carrots, beans and shallots in it. Peel the ginger and grate over these. Wash the chilli, cut in half lengthwise, core, chop finely and add. Season with fish sauce, soy sauce, salt, pepper and lemongrass. Stir in the noodles and allow it all to cool. Divide up onto the sheets of rice paper. Fold the edges over the filling and then roll it all up. Deep fry the rolls in hot oil.

Spicy Filos

Preparation Time: approx. 1 hour

762 kcal/3202 kJ

Serves 4

900 g/2 lb of frozen spinach leaves
oil for the baking sheet
16 sheets of filo pastry
5 shallots
3 cloves of garlic
2 Tbsp butter
100 ml/3 ½ fl oz vegetable stock
salt, pepper
freshly ground nutmeg
3 Tbsp tomato puree
250 g/9 oz feta cheese
2 eggs, 4 Tbsp crème fraîche
100 g/3 ½ oz cubes of white bread
150 g/5 oz melted butter

4 Stir in the tomato puree. Crumble the cheese and stir up with the eggs and crème fraîche. Fold into the spinach together with the cubed bread and put on one side. Lay two pastry sheets flat on a work surface and spread the melted butter on them.

5 Lay 7 further sheets onto each and again spread well with butter. Place half the spinach mixture onto each pastry base. Fold over the edges and carefully roll each one up.

1 Allow the spinach to defrost. Pre-heat the oven to 180 °C/ 355 °F/gas mark 4. Brush a baking sheet thoroughly with oil. Lay the sheets of pastry out next to each other and cover with a damp tea towel.

2 Peel the shallots and dice. Peel the cloves of garlic and chop finely. Heat the butter in a pan and lightly cook the shallots together with the garlic in it.

3 Add the spinach, warm briefly and then pour over the vegetable stock. Allow to simmer for about 4 minutes. Season with salt, pepper and nutmeg.

6 Coat both rolls again with butter and place onto a baking sheet with the seam underneath. Then bake in the oven on the middle shelf for about 20 minutes until golden brown. Finally allow to stand for 5 minutes, cut each one into 4 slices and serve warm.

Mushroom Ravioli

Preparation Time: approx. 45 minutes

767 kcal/3223 kJ

Serves 4

300 g/10 ½ oz plain flour
3 eggs
2 Tbsp oil
salt
flour for rolling out
50 g/1 ¾ oz of dried porcini mushrooms
125 ml/4 ½ fl oz of red wine
600 g/1 lb 5 oz of button mushrooms
4 shallots
2 cloves of garlic
1 bunch of parsley
1 Tbsp of truffle oil
2 Tbsp of olive oil
pepper
250 g of ricotta
100 ml/3 ½ fl oz of mushroom stock
3 Tbsp of butter
2 Tbsp of chopped sage
150 g/5 oz of grated Parmesan cheese

Variation

Fresh radish, peas and some Chinese leaf also make a very good filling. The addition of two cloves of garlic gives the seasoning of this combination that little extra.

1 Sieve the flour onto a work surface. Make a well in the middle and place the eggs, oil and salt in it. Gradually knead the flour into the middle. Work into a smooth dough. Wrap in damp cloth and allow to rest until the filling is ready.

2 Soften the porcini mushrooms by steeping in the red wine. Clean the button mushrooms and cut into small pieces. Peel the shallots and dice. Peel the cloves of garlic and put through a garlic press. Wash the parsley, dry and chop finely. Drain the porcini mushrooms (keeping the liquid) and press slightly to drain the excess juice out.

3 Heat the oil in a frying pan and lightly cook the mushrooms, shallots, garlic and parsley in it. Season with salt and pepper. Mix the ricotta with the mushroom stock and the liquid from soaking the porcini mushrooms and fold in.

4 Halve the dough and roll out one half thinly on a floured work surface. Place the filling on this in portions at 5 cm/2 in intervals. Roll out the second half of the dough just as thinly and lay on top. Cut squares out with a pastry wheel.

5 Press the edges of the ravioli together well. Heat water with a little salt in a sufficiently large pan and simmer the ravioli for 8 about minutes in it. Heat the butter in a pan and lightly cook the sage. Take the ravioli out and arrange on plates with the sage butter. Sprinkle them all with cheese and serve.

Roll out the dough thinly.

Place the filling on top.

Cut out the ravioli.

Simmer in salted water.

Herb Pockets au Gratin

Preparation Time: approx. 1 hour and 10 minutes

1325 kcal/5565 kJ

Serves 4

300 g/10 ½ oz buckwheat flour
300 g/10 ½ oz plain flour
salt, 4 eggs, 2 Tbsp oil
200 ml/7 fl oz water
3 slices of granary bread
250 g/9 oz of crème fraîche
250 g/9 oz low fat fromage frais
40 ml/1 ½ fl oz kirschwasser
pepper
ground cumin and coriander
100 g/3 ½ oz of herb butter
½ bunch of parsley
½ bunch of basil
½ bunch of tarragon
4 Tbsp of tomato puree
100 g/3 ½ oz of chopped hazelnuts
butter for greasing gratin dishes
250 g/9 oz of grated Appenzell cheese

1 Mix the flour and sieve onto a work surface. Make a well in the middle and place salt, 2 eggs and oil inside. Knead everything into a smooth dough whilst gradually adding the water. Cover the dough and leave to rest for approximately 15 minutes.

2 Crumble the slices of bread and place into a large bowl. Mix the remaining eggs with the crème fraîche and add to the bread. Add the fromage frais and kirschwasser to this and season it all with salt, pepper, ground cumin and coriander.

3 Melt the herb butter. Wash the herbs, chop finely and toss in the butter. Add the tomato purée and hazelnuts and allow to sweat for another 3 minutes. Add to the bread and crème fraîche mixture.

4 Divide the dough into 2 portions. Roll out the first half thinly on a floured work surface. Place the herby fromage frais filling on this in portions at 10 cm/ 4 in intervals. Cover the whole thing with the other half of the dough which has likewise been rolled out thinly.

5 Cut a circle round each portion of the filling and fold over. Decorate the edges with the back of a fork. Allow the herb pockets to simmer for about 10 minutes in slightly salted water. Take out and allow to drain.

6 Grease small gratin dishes with butter and place 4-6 pockets in each and sprinkle with the cheese. Cook them all under the grill for about 6 minutes until golden brown. A colourful salad is a good accompaniment to this.

Cabbage Bites with Goat's Cheese

Preparation Time: approx. 50 minutes

990 kcal/4158 kJ

Serves 4

10 leaves of puff pastry (450 g/1 lb)
600 g/1 lb 5 oz white cabbage
250 g/9 oz pearl onions
4 Tbsp walnut oil
1 Tbsp brown sugar
salt
pepper
1 tsp of caraway seeds
125 ml/4 ½ fl oz of strong ale
500 g/1 lb 2 oz of goat's cheese with garlic
1 egg yolk
caraway seeds, poppy seeds
coarse sea salt

1 Allow puff pastry to defrost as per instructions on the packet. Clean and wash the cabbage and slice. Peel the onions and halve.

2 Heat the oil with the sugar in a frying pan and brown the onions in it. Add the cabbage and season with salt, pepper and caraway.

3 Pour in the ale and allow to simmer for about 12 minutes, stirring thoroughly. Crumble the goat's cheese and fold in.

4 Roll out the pastry on a work surface and cut in half. Cut out circles with a diameter of about 8 cm/3 in. Pre-heat the oven to 180 °C/355 °F/gas mark 4.

5 Distribute the filling onto half the number of the circles and cover with the remaining circles. Press together lightly. Paint the pastry with the egg yolk and sprinkle each one with either caraway seeds or poppy seeds or coarse salt.

6 Bake them all in the oven on the middle shelf for about 15 minutes.

TIP

Goat's cheese does not have to have a strong taste. In the meantime you can get it in many variations – from mild cream cheese with or without herbs to hard cheese.

Filled Pancakes

Preparation Time: approx. 45 minutes

523 kcal/2196 kJ

Serves 4

2 aubergines
salt
8 tomatoes
1 bunch of spring onions
1 bunch of basil
40 g/1 ½ oz of preserved ginger
3 red chillis
2 Tbsp Chinese five spice
4 Tbsp sesame oil
3 Tbsp soya bean paste
8 eggs
2 Tbsp plain flour
125 ml/4 ½ fl oz sparkling water
pepper
2 Tbsp clarified butter
4 Tbsp curry ketchup
2 Tbsp Worcester sauce
3 Tbsp light soy sauce
2 Tbsp chilli sauce
4 cloves of garlic
oil for deep frying
green salad to serve

1 Clean and wash the aubergines and cut into cubes. Place in a bowl and sprinkle with salt. Allow to draw for 10 minutes. Finally rinse off and allow to drain.

2 Wash the tomatoes, cut a cross into them, submerge briefly in boiling water, place into cold water, skin, core and cut into cubes.

3 Clean and wash the spring onions and cut into fine rings. Wash and dry the basil and chop finely. Drain the ginger and cut into small pieces.

4 Wash the chillis, cut into half lengthwise, core and chop finely. Heat the oil in a frying pan and allow everything to sweat for about 6 minutes with the Chinese five spice and bean paste.

5 Meanwhile mix the eggs with the flour and the sparkling water. Season with salt and pepper.

6 Heat the clarified butter in a frying pan and cook a pancake from a portion of the batter. Then place a portion of the filling in the middle of the pancake and fold together. Fasten with a cocktail stick. Repeat until all the batter is used.

7 Mix the curry ketchup with the other sauces and season to taste with pressed garlic, salt and pepper. Deep fry the rolls in hot oil for about 2 minutes until golden brown. Finally, allow to drain and serve up with the spicy sauce and a green salad.

Stir batter ingredients.

Cook pancakes.

Fasten with cocktail sticks.

Deep fry in hot oil.

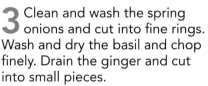

Spicy Strudel Slices

Preparation Time: approx. 50 minutes

882 kcal/3706 kJ

Serves 4

400 g/14 oz ready-made strudel pastry (4 sheets of 100 g/3 ½ oz each)
2 shallots
600 g/1 lb 5 oz oyster mushrooms
1 bunch each of parsley and basil
4 Tbsp walnut oil
salt, pepper
300 g/10 ½ oz of Roquefort cheese
100 g/3 ½ oz of fromage frais
5 Tbsp yoghurt
butter to spread
2 eggs

1 Allow the pastry to defrost according to the instructions on the packet and spread out on a work surface. Sprinkle with water. Peel the shallots and dice. Clean and wash the mushrooms and cut into pieces. Wash and dry the herbs, cut into strips. Heat the oil in a frying pan and lightly fry the shallots with the oyster mushrooms in it. Add the herbs and fry for another 3 minutes. Season to taste with salt and pepper. Pre-heat the oven to 180 °C/355 °F/gas mark 4.

2 Cut the cheese into cubes, mix with the fromage frais and the yoghurt and stir into the mushroom mixture. Spread each sheet of pastry with some butter and then lay one on top of the other. Spread the filling on top. Leave one edge clear. Beat the eggs and spread this edge with the beaten egg. Fold the sides in and then roll the strudel up. Coat the outer surface likewise with egg. Bake the whole thing on the middle shelf of the oven for about 18 minutes.

Filled Baps

Preparation Time: approx. 40 minutes

560 kcal/2352 kJ

Serves 4

450 g/1 lb yeast dough
fat for the baking sheet
2 eggs
4 Tbsp olive oil
cumin seeds for decoration
1 medium cucumber
1 onion
4 cloves of garlic
200 g/7 oz of yoghurt
salt
pepper
1 bunch of dill
1 tsp of vinegar
1 tsp of sugar
8 lettuce leaves

3 Heat the oven to 180 °C/ 355 °F/gas mark 4. Bake on the middle shelf for about 30 minutes. Meanwhile wash the cucumber and slice very finely.

4 Peel the onion and dice. Peel the cloves of garlic and chop finely. Stir the cucumber, onion and garlic into the yoghurt and season to taste with salt and pepper.

5 Wash and dry the dill, chop finely. Mix into the cucumber salad together with the vinegar and the sugar.

6 Cut the lukewarm baps ½ of the way across. Wash and dry the lettuce leaves and line the baps with these. Place the cucumber mixture into them and serve the baps.

1 Allow the dough to defrost and roll out onto a floured work surface. Divide into 4 pieces and shape the pieces into balls.

2 Grease a baking sheet and place the balls on it at a sufficient distance from each other and press flat. Beat the eggs with the oil and spread onto the baps. Sprinkle the cumin seeds on top.

Rice Parcels

Preparation Time: approx. 50 minutes

552 kcal/2194 kJ

Serves 4

4 banana leaves	
250 g/9 oz of red rice	
500 ml/18 fl oz of mushroom stock	
50 g/1 ¾ oz dried morels	
250 g/9 oz tinned artichoke hearts	
200 g/7 oz tinned water chestnuts	
200 g/7 oz tinned palm hearts	
1 onion	
2 cloves of garlic	
6 Tbsp sesame oil	
salt, pepper, ground coriander and cumin	
1 bunch of coriander	
1 Tbsp chopped lemongrass	
oil to coat	

Variation

Instead of the banana leaves, strudel pastry can also be used quite simply. Halve the sheets for this, fold in the sides and roll it all up. Bake through in the oven.

1 Wash, dry and halve the banana leaves. Prepare the rice according to the instructions on the packet in the mushroom stock.

2 Soak the morels in a little water. Allow the artichokes, chestnuts and palm hearts to drain in a sieve. Then cut into small pieces.

3 Peel the onion and dice. Peel the garlic cloves and chop finely.

4 Heat the sesame oil in a frying pan and fry the artichokes, water chestnuts, palm hearts, onion and garlic in it. Season with salt, pepper, ground coriander and cumin.

5 Wash the coriander, dry and then detach the leaves. Add the coriander and the lemongrass to the mixture in the frying pan and allow it all to draw for 3 minutes.

6 Then mix everything with the rice. Place portions of it onto the banana leaves and fold the sides over. Finally roll up.

7 Place all the parcels into a steamer basket with the seam underneath, coat lightly with some oil and allow to steam for about 15 minutes. Open the parcels for serving.

Halve the banana leaves.

Divide the filling.

Fold over the sides.

Place the parcels into the basket.

Coat with some oil.

Magnificently Wrapped: Meat

Meat for once not simply in one piece but wrapped deliciously and originally! Whether rolled up, puréed or minced, in hearty brioches, spicy tacos or stuffed pancakes: experience pork, beef, lamb or game in a completely new way – you can guarantee that taste and creativity have no bounds with our recipes.

Mini Game Tarts

Preparation Time: approx. 45 minutes

685 kcal/2817 kJ

Serves 4

24 ready made mini tarts
2 yellow peppers
1 red pepper
2 cloves of garlic
4 Tbsp lemon juice
1 Tbsp chilli oil
3 Tbsp walnut oil
800 g/1 lb 12 oz of game stewing meat
2 onions
100 g/3 ½ oz frozen vegetables for soup
4 Tbsp clarified butter
125 ml/4 ½ fl oz red wine
100 g/3 ½ oz pickled red cabbage
2 slices of pumpernickel
salt, pepper
ground coriander, cumin and cloves
20 ml/4 tsp gin

1 Prepare the tarts according to the instructions on the packet. Clean and wash the peppers, cut in half, core and dice.

2 Peel the cloves of garlic and chop finely. Purée the peppers, garlic, lemon juice and oil with a hand-held blender.

3 Wash the meat, dry it and put it through the medium disc of the mincer.

4 Peel the onions and dice. Heat the clarified butter in a frying pan and fry the meat with the onions and the defrosted vegetables for soup.

5 After about 4 minutes pour the red wine over it all and add the red cabbage.

6 Crumble the pumpernickel slices and add. Season with salt, pepper, ground coriander, cloves and the gin. Fill the tarts and serve together with the sauce made from the peppers.

Colourful Continental Sausage Brioche

Preparation Time: approx. 1 hour

847 kcal/3559 kJ

Serves 4

1 onion
2 cloves of garlic
2 Tbsp olive oil
20 g/¾ oz frozen herb mix (parsley, dill, mustard cress, chervil, chives)
200 g/7 oz plain wholemeal flour
200 g/7 oz plain flour
2 sachets of dried yeast
1 tsp salt
150 g/5 oz soft herb butter
125 ml/4 ½ fl oz of milk
3 eggs
400 g/14 oz of bierschinken sausage
3 Tbsp of coarse mustard

1 Peel the onions and dice. Peel the cloves of garlic and press. Heat the oil in a frying pan and put the onions, garlic and the defrosted herb mix into it and cook lightly.

2 Knead the flour, yeast, salt, herb butter, milk and eggs into a smooth dough.

3 Knead the onion herb mixture with the dough, cover it all with a cloth and leave to rise for about 15 minutes. Pre-heat the oven to 180 °C/355 °F/gas mark 4. Slice the bierschinken sausage.

4 Roll out the dough on a floured work surface into a rectangle. Distribute the sliced sausage on this and smear with mustard. Fold over the sides and roll it all up. Bake in the oven on the middle shelf for about 25 minutes.

TIP
If you would like something even more substantial you can work diced streaky bacon, which has been pre-cooked, so that the fat has run off into the dough. The brioche also tastes good cold and can therefore be prepared in advance the day before.

Spicy Purses

Preparation Time: approx. 40 minutes

852 kcal/3580 kJ

Serves 4

125 g/4 ½ oz rice flour
125 g/4 ½ oz of plain flour
2 Tbsp groundnut oil
2 tsp salt
125 ml/4 ½ fl oz of sparkling water
400 g/14 oz of veal escallops
250 g/9 oz tinned pineapple pieces
1 bunch of spring onions
4 Tbsp sesame oil
150 g/5 oz of bacon bits
pepper
ground chilli
4 Tbsp mango chutney
3 Tbsp tomato puree
1 bunch of chopped coriander
2 Tbsp chopped walnuts
chive strands for tying up
oil for deep frying
250 g/9 oz tomato pieces
1 bunch of basil
1 Tbsp raspberry vinegar
4 Tbsp olive oil

1 Work the flour together with the oil, salt and sparkling water into a smooth dough. Allow to rest for 10 minutes. Wash and dry the meat, cut into small pieces and then put through the medium disc of the mincer.

2 Allow the pineapple to drain. Clean and wash the onions and cut into rings. Heat the oil in a frying pan and cook the meat lightly together with the bacon bits, pineapple and spring onions. Season with salt, pepper and ground chilli.

3 Mix the chutney with the tomato puree, coriander and walnuts. Add to the meat to briefly warm through and season with salt and pepper.

4 Shape the dough into a roll and cut into 16 portions. Roll all pieces out into circles and divide the meat up between them, placing a portion of the meat into the middle of each. Lift the edge of each circle up all the way round and tie up with a chive strand.

5 Deep fry them all to a golden brown colour in hot oil. Meanwhile stir the tomato pieces with finely chopped basil, vinegar and oil. Season with salt and pepper. Serve with the purses.

Work the dough.

Shape the pastry into a roll.

Lift the edges up.

Tie up with a chive strand.

Caribbean Pancakes

Preparation Time: approx. 45 minutes

805 kcal/3381 kJ

Serves 4

650 g/1 lb 7 oz mixed minced meats
1 Tbsp lemon peel
1 tsp dried thyme
½ tsp dried sage
4 cloves of garlic
3 red onions
6 tsp groundnut oil
salt, pepper, ground chilli
1 mango, 2 onions
½ bunch of mint
2 green chillis
2 Tbsp lemon juice
6 eggs, 4 Tbsp vegetable stock
2 Tbsp cornflour
2 Tbsp clarified butter

1 Mixed up the minced meats with the lemon peel and herbs. Peel the cloves of garlic and press, adding to the mixture. Peel the red onions and dice. Heat the oil in a frying pan and lightly cook the meat with the garlic and onions. Season with salt, pepper and ground chilli.

2 Peel the mango and dice. Peel the onions and likewise dice. Wash the chillis, cut in half lengthwise, core and chop finely. Mix with the lemon juice. Mix the eggs with the vegetable stock and cornflour into a smooth batter.

3 Heat the clarified butter in a frying pan and make a series of pancakes from the batter. Then lay them out onto a work surface. Place some of the meat and mango-onion mixtures onto each and roll up, cut into substantial slices and serve.

Black Pudding Pralines

Preparation Time: approx. 45 minutes

920 kcal/3864 kJ

Serves 4

400 g/14 oz plain flour
200 g/7 oz low fat fromage frais
50 g/1 ¾ oz butter
salt
750 g/1 lb 11 oz smoked black pudding
4 red onions
4 apples
2 Tbsp clarified butter
2 tsp dried marjoram
4 Tbsp of strong ale
pepper
powdered mustard
2 egg yolks for brushing
mustard and horseradish sauce to serve

3 Heat the clarified butter in a frying pan and cook the black pudding lightly with the onions and apples.

4 Add the marjoram and ale, then season it all to taste with salt, pepper and powdered mustard. Pre-heat the oven to 170 °C/340 °F/gas mark 3.

5 Roll the dough out on a floured work surface and cut into rectangles measuring about 12 x 10 cm/5 x 4 in. Place a portion of the black pudding mixture onto each and fold the pastry over it, twisting the ends of the little parcels so that they look like wrapped sweets.

1 Knead the flour, fromage frais and butter together with a pinch of salt into a smooth flaky pastry dough. Then wrap in kitchen foil and chill for 20 minutes.

2 Cut the black pudding into thin strips. Peel the onions and dice. Peel the apples, halve, core and likewise dice.

6 Beat the egg yolks and coat the "sweets" with it. Cook them in the oven on the middle shelf for about 10 minutes. Serve with mustard and some horseradish sauce.

Oriental Tacos

Preparation Time: approx. 35 minutes

917 kcal/3851 kJ

Serves 4

8 tacos
200 g/7 oz tinned chickpeas
200 g/7 oz tinned peas
4 cloves of garlic
2 Tbsp oil
2 Tbsp lemon juice
salt
pepper
600 g/1 lb 5 oz minced lamb
1 bunch of spring onions
3 Tbsp clarified butter
½ tsp each of ground coriander, cumin, cardamom, ginger, clove and cinnamon
1 small sachet of saffron strands
1 bunch of coriander
frisée lettuce leaves
300 g/10 ½ oz natural yoghurt
2 tsp chilli powder

Variation

Instead of the chickpeas and peas use red lentils and sweet corn, cook these through beforehand in some Asian stock. There-after follow the recipe as described.

1 Finish baking the tacos in the oven and keep warm. Drain the chickpeas and peas. Peel the cloves of garlic and press. Put them into a bowl with the oil and, using a hand-held blender, purée it all. Season with lemon juice, salt and pepper.

2 Put the minced lamb through the fine disc of the mincer. Clean the spring onions, wash and cut into rings.

3 Heat the clarified butter in a frying pan and fry the minced lamb in this together with the onions. Season with the salt, pepper, ground coriander, cumin, cardamom, ginger, cloves and cinnamon. Stir in the saffron strands.

4 Wash and dry the coriander and then detach the leaves. Add them to the meat together with the pea mixture and allow to cook for a further 3 minutes.

5 Wash and dry the lettuce leaves. Line the tacos with the leaves and divide the filling between them.

6 Mix the yoghurt with the chilli powder and season with salt and pepper. Arrange the tacos with the sauce on plates and serve.

Purée chickpeas, peas and garlic.

Fry the meat and onions.

Add the pea mixture.

Line the tacos with the lettuce.

Add the filling.

49

Small Pizza Pockets

Preparation Time: approx. 1 hour

777 kcal/3265 kJ

Serves 4

450 g/1 lb frozen yeast dough
2 fennel bulbs
200 g/7 oz tinned artichoke hearts
250 g/9 oz mange tout
200 g/7 oz celery
4 cloves of garlic
300 g/10 ½ oz piece of mortadella
4 Tbsp olive oil
salt, pepper
2 Tbsp dried Italian herbs
3 Tbsp tomato puree
200 g/7 oz grated Pecorino cheese
fennel seeds to sprinkle
plain flour
beer for brushing

1 Allow the dough to defrost according to the instructions on the packet. Clean and wash the fennel bulbs, cut into fine strips. Chop the greenery finely.

2 Let the artichoke hearts drain and then dice. Clean and wash the mange tout and the celery and cut into pieces.

3 Peel the cloves of garlic and chop finely. Cut the mortadella into small cubes. Heat the oil in a frying pan and lightly cook the vegetables in it together with the garlic and the chopped mortadella. Season with salt, pepper, herbs and tomato puree. Allow to cool and mix in the cheese.

4 Pre-heat the oven to 200 °C/390 °F/gas mark 6. Roll the dough out thinly onto a floured work surface and cut into 8 circles with a diameter of about 12 cm/5 in.

5 Line a baking sheet with baking paper and lay 4 circles onto it. Place some filling onto each one and then cover with the remaining circles.

6 Turn the edges up and over and sprinkle them all with some flour and the fennel seeds. Bake in the oven on the middle shelf for about 17 minutes. 5 minutes before the end of the baking time, brush them all with some beer so that the crust becomes nice and crisp.

Filled Ears

Preparation Time: approx. 50 minutes

1485 kcal/6237 kJ

Serves 4

450 g/1 lb of frozen puff pastry
4 red onions, 2 avocados
2 Tbsp lemon juice
2 dried chillis
4 cloves of garlic, 3 Tbsp olive oil
900 g/2 lb of minced lamb
4 Tbsp of spicy ketchup
2 Tbsp of hot mustard
2 tsp Worcester sauce
100 g/3 ½ oz frozen 8-herb mix
salt, pepper
3 Tbsp of breadcrumbs
100 g/3 ½ oz of pepper butter

1 Pre-heat the oven to 180 °C/ 355 °F/gas mark 4. Defrost the puff pastry according to the instructions on the packet. Peel the onions and dice. Halve the avocados, remove the stones, and peel the halves, cut into cubes and drizzle the lemon juice over them. Crumble the dried chillis. Peel the cloves of garlic and chop finely. Heat the oil in a frying pan and lightly cook the onions, avocados, chillis and garlic in it. Add the minced lamb and allow to cook for 4 minutes. Season with the ketchup, mustard, Worcester sauce, herbs, salt and pepper. Stir in the breadcrumbs and allow to continue cooking for a further 3 minutes.

2 Roll out the dough into a large sheet. Distribute the filling over it, leaving an edge of about 2 cm/1 in. Roll up the dough towards the centre from both the long sides. Cut the "ears" off with a knife to a width of about 3 cm/2 in. Brush with the pepper butter and bake in the oven on the middle shelf for 13 minutes until golden brown.

TIP

The ears look very pretty arranged on a bed of nasturtium flowers.

Gourmet Nests

Preparation Time: approx. 55 minutes

685 kcal/2877 kJ

Serves 4

| 400 g/14 oz filo pastry sheets |
| 750 g/1 lb 11 oz of venison fillet |
| 400 g/14 oz of button mushrooms |
| 1 bunch of spring onions |
| ½ bunch each of parsley and thyme |
| 1 sprig of rosemary |
| 2 Tbsp of clarified butter |
| salt, pepper |
| 1 tsp of orange peel essence |
| 4 Tbsp of cranberry jelly |
| 1 Tbsp of sea buckthorn puree |
| 3 Tbsp of red wine |
| 2 Tbsp of crushed green peppercorns |
| butter for the moulds |
| 4 pears |
| 250 g/9 oz of Roquefort cheese |
| Cumberland and mint sauces to serve |

1 Allow the pastry to defrost according to the instructions on the packet. Wash and dry the meat and cut into small cubes.

2 Clean and wash the mushrooms and likewise cut small. Clean and wash the spring onions and cut into rings.

3 Wash and dry the herbs and chop finely. Heat the clarified butter in a frying pan and lightly cook the meat, mushrooms and spring onion in it. Add the herbs and season it all with the salt, pepper, orange peel essence, cranberry jelly, sea buckthorn puree, red wine and peppercorns. Allow to cook for 5 minutes.

4 Pre-heat the oven to 170 °C/ 340 °/gas mark 3. Grease 8 ovenproof cups with the butter. Cut 16 dessert plate-sized large circles out of the pastry. Place two circles into each of the cups and arrange the edge in waves when doing so.

5 Put the filling in them. Peel the pears, halve, core and slice in segments lengthwise and place on top of the filling.

6 Crumble up the cheese with a fork and sprinkle over them. Bake for about 15 minutes in the oven on the middle shelf. Serve with Cumberland sauce and mint sauce.

Grease the cups with butter.

Cut out the pastry circles.

Put into the cups.

Crush the cheese.

Hearty Salad Parcels

Preparation Time: approx. 40 minutes

717 kcal/3013 kJ

Serves 4

800 g/1 lb 12 oz of veal escalope	
4 Tbsp of groundnut oil	
250 g/9 oz of tinned chestnuts	
4 shallots	
3 cloves of garlic	
3 Tbsp of pine nuts	
½ bunch of basil, parsley, oregano	
salt	
pepper	
3 Tbsp of ready-made red pesto	
3 Tbsp of cognac	
12 leaves of lollo rosso lettuce	
chive strands for tying up parcels	
4 slices of toast bread	
100 g/3 ½ oz truffle butter	

1 Wash and dry the meat and cut into fine strips. Heat the oil in a frying pan and fry the strips of meat in this for about 5 minutes.

2 Allow the chestnuts to drain and cut into small pieces. Peel the shallots and dice. Peel the cloves of garlic, chop finely and add to the meat together with the shallots, chestnuts and pine nuts. Wash and dry the herbs, chop finely and likewise add to the mixture. Allow to cook for a further 3 minutes. Season the whole lot with salt, pepper, pesto and cognac.

3 Wash and dry the lettuce leaves and spread out on a work surface. Distribute the filling between them and fold the lettuce leaves together making a parcel.

4 Fasten with chive strands. Toast the bread, cut into triangles, spread with truffle butter and serve with the parcels.

Fajitas

Preparation Time: approx. 45 minutes

842 kcal/3538 kJ

Serves 4

12 small wheat tortillas
1 bunch of spring onions
1 red and 1 yellow pepper
6 cloves of garlic
900 g/2 lb of steak tartar
lemon juice
2 Tbsp of chopped oregano
1 tsp of ground cumin
salt
2 tsp of coarsely ground black pepper
8 plum tomatoes
1 onion
1 bunch of coriander
2 ripe avocados
1 Tbsp chilli oil
4 Tbsp groundnut oil
crème fraîche to serve

3 Mix the meat with the spring onions, peppers and garlic and season with lemon juice, oregano, ground cumin, salt and pepper. Allow to stand for 20 minutes in the refrigerator for the flavours to develop.

4 Wash the tomatoes and dice. Peel the onions and dice. Place the tomatoes and the onion in a bowl. Wash the coriander, dry, chop finely and add.

5 Wash the avocados, halve, remove the stones, peel the halves and cut into pieces. Add to the tomatoes and purée with a hand-held blender. Season to taste with salt and pepper.

1 Prepare the tortillas in the oven as per the instructions on the packet and keep warm. Clean and wash the spring onions, then cut into rings.

2 Wash the peppers and halve, core and dice. Peel the garlic cloves and put through a garlic press.

6 Heat the oil in a frying pan and fry the meat-vegetable mixture in it for about 6 minutes. Spread out the tortillas and place the filling on them, fold up so that they look like cones. Serve with crème fraîche.

Rice Rolls

Preparation Time: approx. 45 minutes

435 kcal/1827 kJ

Serves 4

4 sheets of rice pastry
500 g/1 lb 2 oz of pork fillet
250 g/9 oz of crayfish meat from the chill cabinet
250 g/9 oz of shiitake mushrooms
200 g/7 oz of tinned water chestnuts
4 Tbsp of sesame oil
3 Tbsp of chopped chives
2 Tbsp of chopped lemongrass
2 Tbsp of fish sauce
2 Tbsp of soy sauce
2 Tbsp of chilli sauce
½ bunch of mint
oil for deep frying

1 Cover the pastry sheets with a damp cloth so that they become soft. Wash and dry the meat and cut into small pieces.

2 Chop the crayfish meat finely. Clean and wash the mushrooms, dry and cut into small pieces. Drain the water chestnuts and chop finely.

3 Heat the oil in a frying pan and lightly cook the meat, crayfish meat, mushrooms, chestnuts, chives and lemongrass. Season with fish, soy and chilli sauces. Allow to cook for 5 minutes.

4 Wash the mint and dry, cut into strips and add to the meat. Place some of the filling on each sheet of pastry.

5 Fold in the sides, roll up the parcels and deep fry to a golden brown colour in hot oil. Then allow to drain and serve.

Variation

Do not fold in at the sides but only roll up and steam for 5 minutes in the steamer basket.

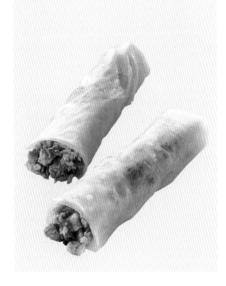

Cover the pastry with damp cloth.

Fry the vegetables and meat.

Place the filling onto the pastry.

Fold the sides over.

Roll everything up.

Empanadas

Preparation Time: approx. 45 minutes

1097 kcal/4609 kJ

Serves 4

450 g/1 lb of frozen puff pastry
150 g/5 oz cut of sliced smoked tongue
1 onion
3 Tbsp clarified butter
350 g/12 oz minced meat
salt
pepper
allspice
ground cumin
2 Tbsp paprika paste
200 g/7 oz of tinned okra
1 bunch of parsley
100 g/3 ½ oz black pitted olives
4 tomatoes
1 green pepper
1 bunch of spring onion
4 cloves of garlic
1 bunch of coriander
1 green chilli
2 Tbsp lemon juice
400 g/14 oz yoghurt
1 egg yolk to coat

1 Defrost the puff pastry according to the instructions on the packet. Lay the discs onto a work surface. Dice the tongue. Peel the onion and likewise dice.

2 Heat the clarified butter in a frying pan and lightly cook the minced meat in it. Add the onion and the tongue and season everything with salt, pepper, allspice, ground cumin and paprika paste.

3 Allow the okra to drain, cut into small pieces and add. Allow to simmer for another 4 minutes. Wash and dry the parsley, chop finely.

4 Allow the olives to drain and cut up into small pieces. Add both to the meat and allow to heat through.

5 Clean and wash the tomatoes and dice. Clean and wash the pepper, halve, core and dice. Clean and wash the spring onions and cut into rings.

6 Peel the cloves of garlic and put through a garlic press. Wash and dry the coriander and chop the leaves finely. Mix together the tomatoes, pepper, spring onions, garlic, coriander, chilli with lemon juice and yoghurt and then season with salt and pepper.

7 Pre-heat the oven to 180 °C/ 355 °F/gas mark 4. Fill half of each disc of pastry with a portion of the filling.

8 Brush the edge of the pastry with water and fold the other half over it to close. Press the edges together and brush with the egg yolk.

9 Then bake in the oven on the middle shelf for about 20 minutes. Serve the empanadas with the yoghurt salsa.

Viennese Mini Croissants

Preparation Time: approx. 40 minutes

1855 kcal/7791 kJ

Serves 4

Ready-made croissant pastry sufficient for 12 small croissants
1 bunch of spring onions
1 bunch of oregano
250 g/9 oz fromage frais
5 Tbsp cream
3 Tbsp horseradish sauce
salt
pepper
paprika
24 small wiener sausages
150 ml/¼ pint ketchup
150 ml/¼ pint chilli sauce
8 cornichons
1 tsp Worcester sauce

1 Heat the oven to 170 °C/ 340 °F/gas mark 3. Spread the croissant pastry out on a floured work surface. Clean and wash the spring onions and cut into rings. Wash and dry the oregano, chop finely.

2 Mix the spring onions with the oregano, fromage frais, cream and 2 Tbsp of horseradish. Season to taste with salt, pepper and paprika. Spread the mass onto the pieces of dough. Allow the sausages to drain and lay two onto each piece of pastry. Roll up the whole thing and bake in the oven on the middle shelf for about 15 minutes.

3 Meanwhile mix the ketchup with the chilli sauce. Allow the cornichons to drain, dice and mix with the rest of the horseradish sauce and Worcester sauce. Arrange the croissants with the sauce on plates and serve.

TIP
You may find frozen croissant pastry handy. If you do not use it all up, you can keep it for a while in the refrigerator.

Temaki-Sushi

Preparation Time: approx. 35 minutes

602 kcal/2530 kJ

Serves 4

400 g/14 oz sushi rice
salt
10 Nori leaves
wasabi paste for brushing
20 lettuce leaves
200 g/7 oz of smoked salmon
50 g/1 ¾ oz of cottage cheese

1 Prepare the rice as per the instructions on the pack in lightly salted water. Dry fry the Nori leaves in a frying pan without fat. Then lay them onto a work surface and cut in half. From each half leaf cut about 3 cm/1 ¾ in and lay a table tennis size ball of rice on the leaf. Spread the rice out flat.

2 Then spread some wasabi paste on top. Lay a washed lettuce leaf on it in such a way that it protrudes somewhat in one corner. Distribute the salmon and the cheese on top.

3 Roll it all up in such a way that a small pointed cone results and that the filling peeps out. The last part of the Nori leaf is stuck down with some grains of rice.

Dry fry the Nori leaves.

Lay a rice ball on each.

Distribute salmon and cheese.

Roll everything up.

Peppercorn Triangles

Preparation Time: approx. 45 minutes

1145 kcal/4846 kJ

Serves 4

240 g/8 ½ oz flour
salt
1 tsp paprika
120 g/4 ¼ oz pepper butter
2 egg yolks
1 Tbsp crème fraîche
500 g/1 lb 2 oz mixed minced meat
2 Tbsp hot mustard
2 Tbsp Worcester sauce
3 cloves of garlic
2 red peppers
1 Tbsp of pickled green peppercorns
5 Tbsp grated cheddar cheese
4 Tbsp chilli oil

1 Work the flour, salt, paprika, butter egg yolk and crème fraîche into a standard dough and allow to rest for about 10 minutes.

2 Mix the minced meat with mustard and Worcester sauce. Peel the cloves of garlic and press, adding the garlic to the meat mixture.

3 Wash the peppers, halve, core and dice. Mix in the chopped peppers, peppercorns and cheese.

4 Heat the oil in a frying pan and fry the meat in it for about 6 minutes. Roll the dough out and cut out 20 squares of about 10 x 10 cm/4 x 4 in. Place a portion of the meat mixture onto each.

5 Brush the edges with a little water and fold the pastry into triangles. Press the edges together and bake in the oven on the middle shelf for about 17 minutes. A colourful salad would go with this.

Savoury Profiteroles

Preparation Time: approx. 45 minutes

610 kcal/2562 kJ

Serves 4

40 g/1 ½ oz of butter	
salt	
1 tsp dried thyme	
1 tsp dried basil	
½ tsp dried rosemary	
120 g/4 ¼ oz plain flour	
200 ml/7 fl oz water	
3 eggs	
1 pinch of baking powder	
150 g/5 oz streaky bacon	
150 g/5 oz pork	
150 g/5 oz veal	
150 g/5 oz boiled ham	
2 shallots	
2 cloves of garlic	
150 g/5 oz of chicken livers	
4 Tbsp of clarified butter	
3 Tbsp of brandy	
pepper	
3 Tbsp of breadcrumbs for frying	
2 Tbsp of double cream	

3 Pre-heat the oven to 200 °C/ 390 °F/gas mark 6. Line a baking sheet with baking paper and lay cherry-sized piles of dough onto it. Bake in the oven on the middle shelf for about 15 minutes.

4 Allow the hot profiteroles to cool somewhat. Press a hole into their undersides with the nozzle of an icing bag. Wash and dry the streaky bacon, meat and ham and dice.

5 Peel the shallots and likewise dice. Peel the cloves of garlic and chop finely. Wash the livers. Put the meat, shallots and garlic through the coarse disc of the mincer.

6 Heat the clarified butter in a frying pan and fry everything in it. Add the brandy. Season to taste with salt and pepper.

1 Place the butter into a pan, heat and stir in salt, herbs and flour. Pour on the water. Stir until the dough separates from the base of the pan.

2 Place it into a bowl and knead in the eggs and baking powder. Work the dough thoroughly until it is shiny and elastic.

7 Stir in the breadcrumbs and the double cream. Place the mixture into an icing bag, squirt the mixture into the profiteroles and serve garnished with fresh herbs.

Curry Pies

Preparation Time: approx. 45 minutes

342 kcal/1438 kJ

Serves 4

300 g/10 ½ oz flour
2 eggs, ½ tsp salt
1 Tbsp curry powder
2 Tbsp oil
flour to work
250 g/9 oz red lentils
2 carrots
1 stick of celery
400 g/14 oz of pork fillet
100 g/3 ½ oz of bean sprouts
4 Tbsp sesame oil
1 Tbsp Chinese five spice
1 Tbsp of raspberry vinegar
5 Tbsp of tomato sauce
2 Tbsp of Worcester sauce
3 Tbsp light soy sauce
2 tsp black bean paste
2 Tbsp chopped garlic
1 tsp brown sugar
2 Tbsp clarified butter
sweet and sour chilli sauce to serve

Variation

Make the filling out of half and half lamb and veal mince. Then add ratatouille (bought frozen) and serve the pies with Bearnaise sauce (bought ready-made).

1 Sieve the flour into a bowl. Add the eggs, salt, curry and oil and work everything into a smooth dough. Cook the lentils according to the instructions on the packet.

2 Clean and wash the carrots, then dice. Clean and wash the celery and cut into pieces. Wash the meat, dry and dice. Wash the bean sprouts and allow to drain.

3 Heat the oil in a frying pan and brown the meat in it. Add the carrots, celery and bean sprouts.

4 Season to taste with Chinese five spice, raspberry vinegar, tomato sauce, Worcester sauce, soy sauce, bean paste, garlic and sugar.

5 Add the drained red lentils and allow everything to cook together for about 4 minutes.

6 Roll out the pastry on a floured work surface. Cut out circles with a diameter of about 10 cm/4 in. Distribute the filling on half the number of the pastry circles and cover with the rest of the circles. Lightly press the edges together.

7 Heat the clarified butter in a frying pan and fry the curry pies in it on both sides for about 4 minutes each. Serve with sweet-and-sour chilli sauce.

Brown the meat.

Add the vegetables.

Place the filling on the pastry.

Press the edges together.

Fry in clarified butter.

Mince Wraps

Preparation Time: approx. 40 minutes

350 kcal/1470 kJ

Serves 4

1 green pepper
2 onions, 2 cloves of garlic
3 Tbsp chilli oil
500 g/1 lb 2 oz minced beef
5 Tbsp ready-made barbecue sauce
1 Tbsp ready-made chilli sauce
250 g/9 oz tinned sweet corn, salt
1 tsp of ground cumin
12 tortillas (bought ready-made)
200 g/7 oz grated Provolone cheese (if not available use cheddar instead)
2 Tbsp clarified butter
slices of tomato and shredded lettuce to serve

1 Clean and wash the pepper, halve, core and cut into thin strips.

2 Peel the onions and dice. Peel the garlic cloves and put through a garlic press. Heat the chilli oil in a frying pan and fry the vegetables in it with the mince. After about 5 minutes add the barbecue and chilli sauces.

3 Allow the sweet corn to drain. Add to the meat and season to taste with the salt and the ground cumin.

4 Pre-heat the oven to 180 °C/ 355 °F/gas mark 4. Spread the tortillas onto a work surface and put the filling on them.

5 Fold all ends of the tortillas into the middle so that little parcels result. Sprinkle the cheese on top of them.

6 Place the little parcels with the seam on the underneath into a buttered shallow casserole dish and bake them in the oven on the middle shelf for about 25 minutes.

7 Arrange the little parcels with sliced tomato and shredded lettuce and serve.

Crispy Curry Rolls

Preparation Time: approx. 45 minutes

280 kcal/1176 kJ

Serves 4

30 sheets of frozen spring roll pastry
200 g/7 oz of broccoli
3 carrots, 200 g/7 oz frozen peas
800 ml/1 pint 8 fl oz of mushroom stock
250 g/9 oz of button mushrooms
1 onion, 2 cloves of garlic
2 Tbsp of herb butter
400 g/14 oz of minced meat
1 bunch of coriander
2 Tbsp of yellow curry paste
oil for deep frying

1 Allow the pastry sheets to defrost in accordance with the instructions on the packet. Clean and wash the broccoli and separate into florets. Clean the carrots, wash and cut into sticks.

2 Defrost the peas. Heat the stock and blanche the vegetables in it for about 4 minutes. Clean and wash the button mushrooms and cut into pieces. Peel the onions and dice. Peel the cloves of garlic and chop finely.

3 Heat the herb butter in a frying pan and brown the mushrooms with the onion, garlic and mince. Drain the vegetables and add. Wash the coriander, dry and chop finely. Stir into the meat with the curry paste. Then divide the filling between the pastry sheets. Fold the sides in and roll up. Tie up with kitchen string and deep fry in hot oil until golden brown. Cucumber salad is good with this.

TIP
So that the rolls keep their shape, first of all fold the sides in and then roll the whole thing up.

Veal Wellington

Preparation Time: approx. 55 minutes

1022 kcal/4294 kJ

Serves 4

4 sheets of frozen strudel pastry
800 g/1 lb 12 oz veal fillet
2 Tbsp clarified butter
salt
pepper
4 Tbsp port
4 cloves of garlic
250 g/9 oz slivers of roasted hazelnut
3 Tbsp groundnut oil
4 Tbsp orange juice
1 tsp brown sugar
2 bunches of peppermint
½ bunch of thyme
3 Tbsp of breadcrumbs

1 Defrost the strudel pastry according to the instructions on the packet. Wash and dry the meat and cut into four pieces. Heat the clarified butter in a frying pan and fry the meat in it on all sides for about 4 minutes. Season with salt and pepper. Drizzle port over it.

2 Wrap the pieces of meat in aluminium foil and allow to rest. Peel the garlic and finely chop. Mix with salt, slivers of hazelnut, groundnut oil, orange juice and sugar.

3 Wash and dry the herbs, chop finely and put with the garlic. Purée it all with a hand-held blender. Add the breadcrumbs and season it all with salt and pepper.

4 Heat the oven to 190 °C/ 375 °F/gas mark 5. Spread out each sheet of pastry in turn and spread with the pesto, omitting the edges.

5 Lay the meat on top, wrap the sides of the pastry round it and press together firmly.

6 Place the Wellingtons onto a greased baking sheet with the seams on the underside and bake for about 20 minutes on the middle shelf of the oven.

Wrap the meat in aluminium foil.

Mix the ingredients for the pesto.

Place the pesto on the pastry.

Make into a parcel.

Tacos "Margarita"

Preparation Time: approx. 30 minutes

857 kcal/3601 kJ

Serves 4

3 Tbsp clarified butter	
400 g/14 oz minced pork	
40 ml/1 ½ fl oz tequila	
1 Tbsp sugar	
1 green chilli	
1 bunch of coriander	
1 Tbsp of grated lemon peel	
salt	
pepper	
200 g/7 oz of peeled tomatoes	
½ bunch of spring onions	
100 g/3 ½ oz of pitted black olives	
3 avocados	
garlic powder and ground cumin	
16 ready-made taco shells	

1 Heat the clarified butter in a frying pan and brown the meat in it. After 4 minutes add the tequila and sugar. Wash the chilli, halve lengthwise, core and chop finely.

2 Wash and dry the coriander, chop finely and add to the meat together with the chilli, lemon peel, salt, pepper and tomatoes.

3 Clean and wash the spring onions and cut into rings. Drain the olives, halve and likewise add to the meat together with the spring onions.

4 Wash the avocados, halve them, remove the stones, peel the halves and cut into pieces. Add to the meat. Season to taste with garlic powder and ground cumin.

5 Place the filling into the tacos. Warm them all up in the oven on 180 °C/355 °F/gas mark 4 for about 10 minutes. Serve immediately.

Piroschkas

Preparation Time: approx. 45 minutes

1217 kcal/5113 kJ

Serves 4

| 150 g/5 oz spelt flour |
| 150 g/5 oz plain flour |
| ½ tsp salt |
| 250 g/9 oz of roast onion butter |
| 7 Tbsp of ice water |
| 3 Tbsp of clarified butter |
| 400 g/14 oz of minced pork |
| pepper |
| 1 tsp of ground cumin |
| 20 ml/4 tsp gin |
| 200 g/7 oz of mustard gherkins from jar |
| 200 g/7 oz of pickled beetroot |
| 100 g/3 ½ oz pickled pumpkin |
| 100 g/3 ½ oz sunflower seeds |
| 3 slices of pumpernickel |
| paprika |
| milk to brush on |
| poppy seeds for decoration |
| keta caviar and sour cream to serve |

3 Season with salt, pepper and ground cumin. Add the gin. Allow the gherkins, beetroot and pumpkin to drain and then cut into small pieces. Add to the meat together with the sunflower seeds and the crumbled pumpernickel. Season with paprika.

4 Pre-heat the oven to 180 °C/ 355 °F/gas mark 4. Roll out the pastry onto a floured work surface and cut out circles with a diameter of about 12 cm/5 in.

5 Distribute the filling onto them and fold the pastry right over. Press the sides together well and use a fork to press notches round the outer edge.

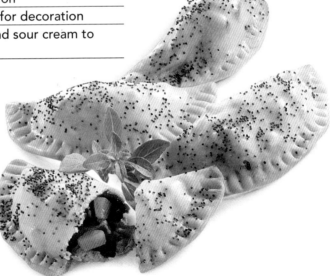

1 Work the flour together with the salt, butter and ice water into a smooth pastry. Allow to rest for 10 minutes.

2 Heat clarified butter in a frying pan and brown the meat in it.

6 Brush the little pasties with milk and sprinkle with poppy seed. Bake in the oven on the middle shelf for about 20 minutes. Serve with caviar and sour cream.

Stuffed Hearted Cabbage

Preparation Time: approx. 40 minutes

360 kcal/1512 kJ

Serves 4

12 medium-sized leaves from a hearted cabbage
salt
300 g/10 ½ oz of hare fillet
100 g/3 ½ oz of smoked dried meat
2 shallots
3 Tbsp clarified butter
1 tsp allspice corns
½ Tbsp dried sage
½ Tbsp dried thyme
pepper
4 Tbsp Madeira
4 Tbsp cranberry purée
3 Tbsp oil
500 ml/18 fl oz game stock
plum sauce to serve

1 Blanche the cabbage leaves in boiling salted water for about 3 minutes. Rinse in ice water.

2 Cut the leaves' ribs flat. Wash and dry the meat and dice.

3 Peel the shallots and dice. Put the meat and shallots through the medium disc of the mincer.

4 Heat the clarified butter in a frying pan and fry the meat with the shallots for about 5 minutes. Add the allspice corns, sage, thyme and pepper. Use Madeira to add aroma to it all.

5 Stir in the cranberry puree. Place some of the stuffing onto each cabbage leaf, fold in the sides and roll up the leaves. Fasten with cocktail sticks.

6 Heat the oil in a frying pan and fry the rolls briefly in this then pour the game stock over them and cook lightly for about 8 minutes. Arrange the stuffed cabbage leaves with plum sauce and serve.

Variation

Use radicchio instead of the hearted cabbage and veal fillet instead of the hare fillet. Stir in tomato puree instead of cranberry puree.

Blanche the cabbage leaves.

Brown the meat.

Put the stuffing on.

Fold in the sides and roll up.

Fasten with cocktail sticks.

73

Bite-Size Refinement: Poultry and Game Birds

Juicy, tender and wonderfully versatile: not only Asian cuisine long knows to treasure poultry and for good reason. Surrounded in noodle dough, wrapped in rolls of pastry or as a spicy filling for peppers or fine puff pastry vol-au-vents you will be gaining fresh honours for chicken, turkey and duck.

Noble Noodle Pockets

Preparation Time: approx. 40 minutes

880 kcal/3696 kJ

Serves 4

600 g/1 lb 5 oz plain flour, 5 eggs
5 Tbsp hazelnut oil, salt
600 g/1 lb 5 oz chicken breast fillets
200 g/7 oz chicken livers
100 g/3 ½ oz of bacon
3 Tbsp pepper butter
pepper, ground coriander, cumin and allspice
3 Tbsp Madeira
2 onions
2 cloves of garlic
2 bunches of parsley
3 Tbsp herb butter

1 Sieve the flour onto a work surface. Make a well in the middle and place the eggs, oil and salt in it. Slowly knead the flour into the middle. Knead it all into a smooth dough, cover and allow to rest for about 10 minutes.

2 Wash the meat, dry and put through the medium disc of the mincer.

3 Chop the bacon finely. Heat the pepper butter in a frying pan and in it brown the meat together with the bacon. Season with salt, pepper, ground coriander, cumin and allspice. Give aroma with the Madeira.

4 Roll out the dough thinly on a floured work surface and cut out circles with a diameter of about 10 cm/4 in.

5 Put portions of the meat mixture onto half of them, leaving a clear edge all round. Brush the edges with water and then cover with the remaining circles. Press the edges together lightly. Allow the pockets to cook in lightly salted water for about 6 minutes.

6 Peel the onions and dice. Peel the cloves of garlic and chop finely. Wash and dry the parsley and chop finely.

7 Heat the butter and lightly cook the onions, garlic and parsley in it. Season with salt and pepper. Arrange the noodle pockets on plates with the herb butter and serve.

Asparagus and Turkey Rolls

Preparation Time: approx. 45 minutes

707 kcal/2971kJ

Serves 4

20 frozen spring roll sheets
500 g/1 lb 2 oz turkey breast fillet
3 Tbsp clarified butter
100 g/3 ½ oz bacon bits
3 Tbsp herbes de Provence
salt
pepper
3 Tbsp brandy
500 g/1 lb 2 oz of green asparagus
600 ml/1 pint 1 fl oz poultry stock
2 Tbsp butter
200 g/7 oz Gorgonzola cheese
oil for deep frying

1 Allow the pastry to defrost according to the instructions on the packet. Spread out onto a work surface. Wash and dry the meat, cut into pieces and then put through the coarse disc of the mincer.

2 Heat the clarified butter in a frying pan and brown the meat in it with the bacon bits. Add the herbs and season it all with salt, pepper and brandy.

3 Clean and wash the asparagus and cut the ends off. Heat the stock with the butter and blanche the asparagus in it for about 4 minutes.

4 Spread the pastry sheets with portions of the meat mixture and divide up the asparagus spears between them. Slice the cheese and lay on top of the asparagus. Fold the dough in at the sides and roll up.

5 Heat the oil in the deep fat fryer and fry the rolls in it until golden brown.

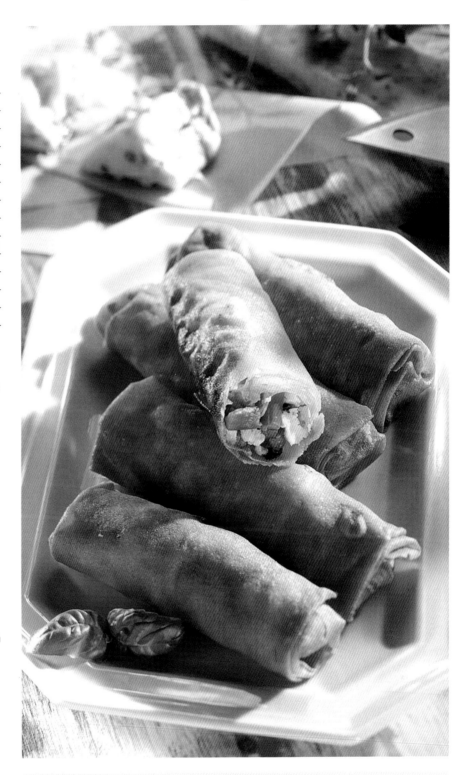

TIP

As accompaniments to the asparagus and turkey rolls, a mixed salad and a sweet-and-sour dip would work well.

Turkey Sticks

Preparation Time: approx. 50 minutes

1250 kcal/5250 kJ

Serves 4

350 g/12 oz plain flour	
350 g/12 oz low fat fromage frais	
250 g/9 oz chilled pepper butter	
1 onion	
2 cloves of garlic	
4 Tbsp of olive oil	
100 g/3 ½ oz of pine nuts	
800 g/1 lb 12 oz turkey breast fillet	
60 g/2 oz of currants	
1 Tbsp chopped parsley	
1 Tbsp chopped basil	
1 Tbsp chopped thyme	
2 egg yolks	

1 Work the flour, fromage frais and pepper butter into a smooth dough. Stand in a cool place for 10 minutes. Peel the onion and dice.

2 Peel the garlic and dice. Heat the oil in a frying pan and lightly cook the onion in it together with the garlic. Add the pine nuts.

3 Wash and dry the meat, cut into small pieces and stir into the onion mixture. Add the currants and herbs and allow to cook for 5 minutes.

4 Heat the oven to 180 °C/ 355 °F/gas mark 4. Roll the puff pastry out on a floured work surface and cut into pieces measuring 9 x 13 cm/3 ½ x 5 in.

5 Divide the meat mixture up between the pieces of pastry. Fold over the sides and roll it all up. Then roughly shape into rectangular parcels.

6 Brush the parcels with egg yolk and bake them in the oven on the middle shelf for about 18 minutes.

Work the dough.

Cut into pieces.

Distribute the meat.

Roll it all up.

Wraps with Shrimps

Preparation Time: approx. 45 minutes

535 kcal/2247kJ

Serves 4

250 g/9 oz maize flour
1 tsp salt
1 tsp each of ground coriander, cumin and ginger
500 ml/18 fl oz milk
3 eggs
4 Tbsp of clarified butter
½ grilled chicken
250 g/9 oz mixed pickles
250 g/9 oz shrimps
200 g/7 oz tinned sweet corn
5 Tbsp ready-made hot salsa
1 bunch of coriander
3 Tbsp butter

1 Work the flour together with the salt, ground coriander, cumin, ginger, milk, eggs and clarified butter into a smooth batter and allow to rest for 10 minutes.

2 Remove the chicken flesh from the bone and cut into pieces. Allow the mixed pickles to drain in a sieve and halve. Wash the shrimps and dry. Likewise drain the sweet corn in a sieve.

3 Stir up the chicken, mixed pickles, shrimps and sweet corn together with the salsa. Wash and dry the coriander, detach the leaves and stir into the salsa.

4 Heat the butter up in a frying pan and cook 12 thin sweet corn flatbreads from portions of the batter. Divide up the filling onto them, fold over the flatbreads and serve immediately.

Green Rolls

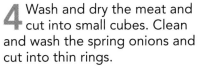

Preparation Time: approx. 55 minutes

490 kcal/2058 kJ

Serves 4

300 g/10 ½ oz of floury potatoes

salt

50 g/1 ¾ oz pepper butter

2 eggs

pepper

½ bunch of parsley

12 large white cabbage leaves

350 g/12 oz chicken breast fillet

1 bunch of spring onions

4 Tbsp olive oil

250 g/9 oz tomatillos

2 carrots

ground cumin

650 ml/1 lb 7 oz poultry stock

sour cream sauce to serve

4 Wash and dry the meat and cut into small cubes. Clean and wash the spring onions and cut into thin rings.

5 Heat the oil in a frying pan and lightly cook the meat and spring onions in it. Wash and dry the tomatillos, remove the skin and dice the flesh of the fruit.

1 Boil the potatoes in their skins in boiling water for about 18 minutes. Then drain, peel and put through the potato press.

2 Work the potato mass together with the pepper butter and eggs into a smooth dough. Season with pepper. Wash and dry the parsley, chop finely and stir in.

3 Blanche the cabbage leaves in lightly salted water for about 3 minutes. Then halve the cabbage leaves and lay on a chopping board.

6 Clean and wash the carrots and cut into batons. Add both to the meat and allow to simmer for another 3 minutes.

7 Place the meat together with the vegetables and the potato mixture into a bowl and mix together. Season to taste with salt, pepper and ground cumin.

8 Divide up between the cabbage leaves, fold in and roll up. Fix with cocktail sticks. Heat up the stock and lay the parcels in it and allow to simmer for 10 minutes on low heat. Serve with a sour cream sauce.

Duck Packets

Preparation Time: approx. 40 minutes

640 kcal/2688 kJ

Serves 4

12 red oak-leaved lettuce leaves
12 sheets of rice paper
450 g/1 lb of skinless duck breast fillet
600 ml/1 pint 1 fl oz poultry stock
250 g/9 oz Chinese leaf
4 shallots
2 cloves of garlic
1 red chilli
2 Tbsp of raspberry vinegar
1 bunch of parsley
1 bunch of basil
salt
pepper
3 Tbsp fish sauce
2 Tbsp light soy sauce
4 Tbsp chopped peanuts
4 Tbsp groundnut oil
mustard cress to serve

1 Wash and dry the lettuce leaves. Wrap the rice paper sheets in damp cloths so that they soften up.

2 Wash and dry the meat and dice. Bring the stock to boil in a pan and allow the meat to cook in it for 15 minutes.

3 Clean and wash the Chinese leaf and cut into fine strips. Peel the shallots and dice. Peel the cloves of garlic and chop finely.

4 Wash and dry the chilli, halve lengthwise, core and chop finely. Allow the meat to drain and place in a bowl with the Chinese leaf, shallots, garlic and chilli. Drizzle raspberry vinegar over it all.

5 Wash and dry the herbs and chop finely. Likewise add and season it all with salt, pepper, fish sauce and soy sauce.

6 Add the peanuts and the groundnut oil. Put the filling onto the lettuce leaves and fold into packets. Wrap them all in the rice paper sheets and arrange on a bed of mustard cress.

Variation

Use rice instead of the meat. Fix the rice paper with cocktail sticks and then deep fry them in hot oil until golden brown.

Wrap up the rice paper.

Cut the Chinese leaf into strips.

Drizzle raspberry vinegar over it all.   Season to taste with the spices.   Fold the lettuce packets together.

Florentine Chicken Triangles

Preparation Time: approx. 1 hour

657 kcal/2761 kJ

Serves 4

250 g/9 oz wholemeal flour

100 g/3 ½ oz of plain flour

100 g/3 ½ oz of grated Parmesan cheese

3 tsp baking powder

1 tsp salt

2 Tbsp fennel seeds

300 g/10 ½ oz low fat fromage frais

200 g/7 oz frozen leaf spinach

300 g/10 ½ oz boned chicken breast

4 red onions

2 cloves of garlic

3 Tbsp oil

2 Tbsp clarified butter

200 g/7 oz peeled tomatos

3 Tbsp red wine

pepper

2 egg yolks

1 Mix the flour together with the Parmesan cheese, baking powder, salt, fennel seeds and fromage frais to a smooth dough and chill for 10 minutes.

2 Defrost the spinach. Cut the meat into narrow strips. Peel the onions and dice.

3 Peel the garlic and chop finely. Heat the oil and clarified butter and brown the onions with the garlic and chicken.

4 Add the tomatoes, spinach and red wine. Allow to simmer for about 4 minutes. Season strongly with salt and pepper.

5 Pre-heat the oven to 180 °C/ 355 °F/gas mark 4. Roll the dough out onto a floured work surface and cut into squares 12 x 12 cm/5 x 5 in.

6 Place portions of the filling into the middle of the squares and fold each one over into a triangular shape. Press the edges together well and decorate them with a fork.

7 Brush the florentine chicken triangles with the egg yolk and bake them in the oven on the middle shelf for about 18 minutes.

Spicy Stuffed Peppers

Preparation Time: approx. 40 minutes

1990 kcal/8358 kJ

Serves 4

8 small peppers
600 g/1 lb 5 oz of poultry bratwurst
200 g/7 oz of oyster mushrooms
1 bunch of basil
1 bunch of parsley
2 cloves of garlic
3 Tbsp of olive oil
salt, pepper, paprika
150 g/5 oz of passata
small tin of mushrooms
50 g/1 ¾ oz pine nuts

1 Wash the peppers, cut lids and core. Squeeze the sausage meat out of the skin.

2 Clean and wash the oyster mushrooms and cut into pieces. Wash and dry the herbs and chop finely.

3 Peel the cloves of garlic and put through the garlic press. Heat the olive oil in a frying pan and lightly cook the sausage meat in it together with the oyster mushrooms, herbs and garlic. Season it all to taste with salt, pepper and paprika.

4 Add the passata, the other mushrooms, which have been chopped finely, and pine nuts. After about 5 minutes cooking time, fill the peppers with the mixture. Place these in a steamer basket and steam for 15 minutes. Arrange on plates and serve.

TIP
A chilled vegetable soup goes with the peppers – in a trice a light meal is ready for hot days.

Turkey Ravioli

Preparation Time: approx. 35 minutes

630 kcal/2646 kJ

Serves 4

350 g/12 oz buckwheat flour	
2 eggs, 5 egg yolks	
3 Tbsp beetroot juice, salt	
400 g/14 oz of turkey breast roll in one piece	
2 Tbsp truffle oil	
100 g/3 ½ oz bacon bits	
1 Tbsp chopped rosemary	
20 g/ ¾ oz of black truffle	
2 Tbsp grappa	
4 Tbsp cream cheese	
pepper, onion and garlic powders	
1 egg white	
truffle butter to serve	

1 Sieve the flour onto a work surface and make a well in the middle. Put in eggs, egg yolks, juice and some salt. Slowly work everything in and knead to a smooth dough. Allow to rest for about 10 minutes.

2 Cut the turkey roll into small cubes. Heat the truffle oil and brown the cubes of turkey with the bacon bits in it. Add the rosemary.

3 Grate the truffle into thin discs and carefully add. Use the grappa to add aroma and stir in the cream cheese. Season it all with salt, pepper, onion and garlic powders.

4 Roll the dough out on a floured work surface and cut out rectangles of about 6 x 12 cm/2 ½ x 5 in. Distribute portions of the filling onto these. Leave one half empty on each and brush this with some egg white.

5 Place the empty half of the dough over the filling and press the edges together. Cook the ravioli for 8 minutes in lightly salted water. Serve with truffle butter.

Sieve the flour onto a surface.

Cut out rectangles.

Brush edges with egg white.

Press the edges together.

Spicy Burritos

Preparation Time: approx. 50 minutes

452 kcal/1900 kJ

Serves 4

800 ml/1 pint 8 fl oz poultry stock
350 g/12 oz frozen brussel sprouts
8 medium sized tortillas
600 g/1 lb 5 oz boned goose breast
250 g/9 oz pearl onions
3 Tbsp clarified butter, 3 Tbsp red wine
½ bunch each of thyme and parsley
salt, pepper
hot dip and salad to serve

1 Heat the poultry stock and blanche the brussel sprouts in it for about 8 minutes. Lift out using a strainer ladle and allow to drain.

2 Cut the brussel sprouts in half. Bake the tortillas in the oven according to the instructions on the packet and keep warm. Remove the skin from the meat. Cut the meat into cubes.

3 Peel the pearl onions and halve. Heat clarified butter in a frying pan and brown the meat in it together with the pearl onions. Use the red wine to give an aroma.

4 Wash and dry the herbs, chop finely and add together with the halved brussel sprouts. Season with salt and pepper and allow to simmer for 4 minutes. Divide up between the tortillas, roll them up and serve with a hot dip and some salad.

Chicken Vol au Vents

Preparation Time: approx. 1 hour

795 kcal/3339 kJ

Serves 4

450 g/1 lb frozen puff pastry	
2 egg whites	
900 g/2 lbs chicken breast fillet	
4 Tbsp clarified butter	
1 Tbsp grated lemon peel	
2 Tbsp lemon juice	
2 mangoes	
3 nectarines	
1 orange	
salt	
pepper	
ground cardamom, coriander, cloves and allspice	
4 Tbsp coconut cream	
3 Tbsp ginger jam	

1 Defrost the pastry according to the instructions on the packet. Lay the sheets of pastry on top of each other and roll out. Cut out 16 circles with a diameter of about 10 cm/4 in each. In 8 of the circles cut out the middle in a circle with a diameter of about 2 cm/1 in.

2 Pre-heat the oven to 180 °C/ 355 °F/gas mark 4. Rinse a baking sheet in cold water and slightly dampen the pastry.

3 Lay a ring onto each of 8 pastry circles and brush the egg white over them all. Lay the lids at the front on the baking sheet.

4 Bake them all in the oven on the middle shelf for about 25 minutes. Take the lids out of the oven slightly earlier as they bake more quickly.

5 In the meantime, wash the meat, dry it and cut into cubes. Heat the clarified butter in a frying pan and brown the meat in it.

6 Add the lemon peel and lemon juice. Peel the mangoes, halve them and de-stone, dice the flesh of the fruit.

7 Cut a cross into the top of the nectarines, dip them briefly into boiling water, remove the skin, de-stone and likewise dice. Peel the orange so that the pith is removed. Cut the stringy bits out.

8 Add the fruit and season it with the spices. Add the coconut cream and jam. Put it all into the warm vol au vents and serve.

Colourful Party Tacos

Preparation Time: approx. 45 minutes

415 kcal/1743 kJ

Serves 4

100 g/3 ½ oz red lentils
500 ml/18 fl oz Asian stock
800 g/1 lb 12 oz of turkey breast fillet
2 tomatoes
½ bunch of spring onions
1 red pepper
3 Tbsp sesame oil
3 Tbsp yellow curry paste
1 Tbsp chopped lemongrass
2 Tbsp light soy sauce
3 Tbsp fish sauce
8 tacos (bought ready-made)
8 lettuce leaves

1 Place the lentils into hot Asian stock and boil for 18 minutes.

2 Wash and dry the meat and cut into strips. Wash and dry the tomatoes and cut into small segments.

3 Clean and wash the spring onions and cut into thin rings. Clean and wash the red pepper, halve, core and cut into strips.

4 Heat the oil in a frying pan and brown the meat in it. Add the tomatoes, spring onions, pepper and drained lentils.

5 Season everything with curry paste, lemongrass, soy sauce and fish sauce. Allow to cook together for about 7 minutes. Briefly heat up the tacos in the oven at 180 °C/355 °F/gas mark 4.

6 Line the tacos with the washed lettuce leaves, put the filling inside and serve up.

Variation

Use kidney beans instead of the lentils which are then browned later with a chilli and 3 cloves of garlic. Then season it all with chilli powder, salt and pepper

Cut the tomatoes into segments.

Cut the pepper into strips.

Brown everything.

Add the lentils.

Put the filling into the tacos.

Lucullus Dumplings

Preparation Time: approx. 55 minutes

747 kcal/3139 kJ

Serves 4

450 g/1 lb plain flour
1 tsp salt
1 tsp paprika
125 ml/4 ½ fl oz sparkling water
125 ml/4 ½ fl oz milk
300 g/10 ½ oz of tinned artichoke hearts
4 shallots
1 clove of garlic
1 bunch of parsley
3 Tbsp olive oil
1 Tbsp lemon juice
2 Tbsp sherry
4 Tbsp tapenade
400 g/14 oz of duck breast fillets
2 Tbsp of breadcrumbs for frying
herb butter to serve

1 Stir flour together with the salt, paprika, sparkling water and milk into a smooth dough. Allow to rest for about 10 minutes.

2 Allow the artichoke hearts to drain in a sieve and cut into small pieces. Peel the shallots and dice. Peel the clove of garlic and dice.

3 Wash and dry the parsley, then chop finely. Heat the oil in a frying pan and in it lightly cook the artichokes together with the shallots, garlic and parsley. Use the lemon juice and sherry to add aroma.

4 Stir in the tapenade, take the pan off the stove and allow to stand. Wash and dry the meat and put through the medium disc of the mincer.

5 Then knead together with the breadcrumbs and the vegetables. Roll out the pastry on a floured surface and cut out about 30 circles with a diameter of 8 cm/3 in each.

6 Shape 30 small balls out of the meat mixture and place in the middle of the dough circles. Press the edges of the dough onto each meat balls in such a way that it looks like a kind of flower which is open at the top. Press the underside of the dough flat.

7 Place the dumplings into a steamer basket and steam for about 12 minutes. Arrange with some herb butter and serve.

Clever Salad Wraps

Preparation Time: approx. 40 minutes

560 kcal/2352 kJ

Serves 4

8 large romaine lettuce leaves
salt
650 g/1 lb 7 oz small green beans
500 ml/18 fl oz poultry stock
4 plum tomatoes
½ bunch of spring onions
½ grilled chicken
250 g/9 oz of tinned crayfish
pepper
4 egg yolks
2 Tbsp mustard
125 ml/4 ½ fl oz hazelnut oil
125 ml/4 ½ oz truffle oil
1 Tbsp lemon juice
8 quail eggs from a jar

1 Wash the lettuce leaves and blanch for 3 minutes in lightly salted water. Cut in half. Wash the beans and allow to cook in the stock for about 8 minutes. Clean and wash the tomatoes and dice. Clean and wash the spring onions and cut into rings. Remove the chicken from the bone and cut into small pieces. Allow the crayfish to drain and cut into pieces.

2 Pour the water off and drain the beans. Cut into pieces. Stir the beans, tomatoes, spring onions, chicken and crayfish meat in a bowl and season with pepper. Stir the egg yolks with salt, pepper and mustard. Gradually stir in the oil. Add the lemon juice. Pour the mayonnaise over the mixture of meat and vegetables and mix everything together carefully. Cut the quail eggs into 4 and add. Divide up the mixture between the leaf halves, fold in the sides and roll it all up.

TIP
Arrange the wraps in a star shape on an edible tray made from puff pastry with edible flowers.

Napoleons with Goose Mousse

Preparation Time: approx. 40 minutes

972 kcal/4084 kJ

Serves 4

250 g/9 oz frozen puff pastry
2 egg yolks
200 g/7 oz of smoked goose breast
100 g/3 ½ oz of goose liver pâté
4 Tbsp port
salt
2 Tbsp pickled peppercorns
100 g/3 ½ oz of frozen herbes de Provence
250 ml/9 fl oz double cream

1 Defrost the puff pastry according to the instructions on the packet. Pre-heat the oven to 200 °C/390 °F/gas mark 6. Lay 2 sheets of the pastry over each other and press lightly together. Divide the sheets into 4 equally large rectangles. Cut 2 strips off the side of each rectangle. Lay the dough strands lengthwise over the dough sheets and brush it all with egg yolk. Bake everything in the oven on the middle shelf for about 18 minutes.

2 Dice the goose breast roughly and place in a bowl together with the pâté and the port and stir. Season it all with salt and the crushed peppercorns. Add the defrosted herbs. Whip the cream until stiff and carefully stir into the mixture. Allow everything to chill thoroughly.

3 Cut the puff pastry slices in half lengthwise and spread the mixture on the bottom half. Put the other half back on top and serve up.

Cut the dough into rectangles.

Cut strips off sides.

Lay lengthwise on the dough.

Halve the pastry slices.

Alsatian Crepe Rolls

Preparation Time: approx. 40 minutes

880 kcal/3696 kJ

Serves 4

4 Tbsp butter
4 eggs
125 g/4 ½ oz wholemeal flour
125 g/4 ½ oz plain flour
salt
250 ml/9 fl oz milk
250 ml/9 fl oz sparkling water
4 red onions
2 bunches of spring onions
400 g/14 oz of poultry salami
3 Tbsp of walnut oil
300 g/10 ½ oz sauerkraut
4 Tbsp cider
pepper
½ Tbsp caraway seeds
1 pinch of ground cardamom
3 Tbsp clarified butter

1 Mix the butter up with the eggs, flour, salt, milk and sparkling water and allow the batter to rest for 10 minutes.

2 Peel the onions and dice. Clean and wash the spring onions and cut into rings. Dice the salami.

3 Heat the oil in a frying pan and lightly cook the onions, spring onions and salami in it. Add the sauerkraut and pour the cider over it all. Season with salt, pepper, caraway seeds and ground cardamom.

4 Heat the clarified butter in a frying pan and make crepes out of portions of the batter. Then spread with the filling, roll up and serve warm.

Poultry Tamalas

Preparation Time: approx. 50 minutes

552 kcal/2320 kJ

Serves 4

| 24 dried maize leaves |
| 200 g/7 oz tinned sweet corn |
| 600 ml/1 pint 1 fl oz poultry stock |
| salt |
| pepper |
| 500 g/1 lb 2 oz chicken breast fillet |
| 2 Tbsp clarified butter |
| 200 g/7 oz portabello mushrooms |
| 100 g/3 ½ oz pearl onions |
| 125 ml/4 ½ fl oz dry sparkling wine |
| 4 sprigs of thyme |
| 1 sprig of rosemary |
| 1 bunch of flat-leaved parsley |

3 Clean and wash the mushrooms and cut into small pieces. Peel the pearl onions and chop finely.

4 Add both these to the meat with the sparking wine. Wash and dry the thyme and rosemary, detach the leaves and chop finely. Likewise add to the meat. Allow everything to cook for about 4 minutes and season with salt and pepper. Add the sweet corn.

1 Place the maize leaves in water for about 5 minutes. Allow the maize to drain in a sieve and allow to cook in the vegetable stock for about 4 minutes. Season with salt and pepper.

2 Wash and dry the meat and cut into strips. Heat the clarified butter in a frying pan and brown the meat in it on all sides. Season with salt and pepper.

5 Lay two leaves over each other crossways each time, place a portion of the filling in the middle, fold the leaves in and fix with a cocktail stick. Place the tamalas, with the seam on the underside, into a steamer basket and steam for about 20 minutes.

6 Then open up the leaves and arrange onto a plate decoratively and serve.

Guinea Fowl Triangles

Preparation Time: approx. 55 minutes

545 kcal/2289 kJ

Serves 4

16 filo pastry sheets
800 g/1 lb 12 oz guinea fowl breast
250 g/9 oz chicken livers
2 fennel bulbs
2 cloves of garlic
2 dried chillis
4 Tbsp of olive oil
3 Tbsp frozen herbes de Provence
1 slice of grated toast bread
20 ml/4 tsp red wine
salt
pepper
butter to spread

Variation

Shape little envelopes instead of the triangles and do this by cutting the filo sheets into squares. Place the filling in the middle, pull the corners over and press together.

1 Lay out the filo sheets next to each other and cover them all with a damp tea towel. Pre-heat the oven to 180 °C/ 355 °F/gas mark 4.

2 Wash the meat and the livers and put through the coarse disc of the mincer.

3 Clean and wash the fennel and cut into strips. Chop the greenery finely. Peel the cloves of garlic and put through the garlic press. Crumble up the chillis.

4 Heat the oil in a frying pan and brown the meat with fennel, the fennel greenery, garlic, chillis and herbs.

5 Add the toast bread and give it aroma with the red wine. Season with salt and pepper.

6 Halve each filo sheet lengthwise and place a portion of the filling on one half of each resulting sheet. Fold the other half over it and then fold in such a way that a triangle results.

7 Place the triangle with the seam underneath on a baking sheet which has been lined with baking paper. Brush with butter and bake on the middle shelf for about 20 minutes.

Cut the fennel into strips.

Brown everything in the oil.

Halve the filo sheets.

Place the mixture onto the pastry.

Fold it all into triangles.

Herby Turkey Parcels

Preparation Time: approx. 45 minutes

567 kcal/2383 kJ

Serves 4

8 thin turkey fillets
salt
pepper
1 apple
6 shallots
300 g/10 ½ oz pork sausage meat
1 Tbsp chilli sauce
ground allspice, cinnamon, aniseed and cumin
3 Tbsp chopped walnuts
½ bunch of basil
2 sprigs of thyme
butter for greasing
some sage leaves
some rosemary needles
180 ml/6 fl oz calvados

1 Wash and dry the meat and season with salt and pepper. Peel the apple, halve, core and dice.

2 Peel the shallots and dice. Place the apple and shallots into a bowl with the sausage meat and season with the chilli sauce, salt, pepper, ground allspice, cinnamon, aniseed and cumin.

3 Pre-heat the oven to 200 °C/ 390 °F/gas mark 6. Coat the fillets with the mixture and decorate with the chopped walnuts. Roll up and fix with cocktail sticks.

4 Wash the basil and chop finely. Wash the thyme and detach the leaves. Grease 8 pieces of aluminium foil with some butter and distribute the herbs between them. Dribble the calvados on them, lay the rolls on them and roll up inside the foil.

5 Bake all of them in the oven on the middle shelf for about 20 minutes. Open the aluminium foil and arrange decoratively with the foil and serve.

Crispy Flautas

Preparation Time: approx. 35 minutes

747 kcal/3139 kJ

Serves 4

8 medium-sized ready-made tortillas
600 g/1 lb 5 oz chicken breast fillet
600 g/1 lb 5 oz surimi
2 Tbsp green peppercorns
4 Tbsp olive oil
250 g/9 oz antipasti from a jar
2 Tbsp ready-made pesto
salt
pepper
200 g/7 oz grated Pecorino cheese

1 Prepare the tortillas in the oven according to the instructions on the packet and keep warm. Wash and dry the meat and surimi, chop into small pieces. Pre-heat the oven to 180 °C/ 355 °F/gas mark 4.

2 Crush the peppercorns. Heat the oil in a frying pan and in it lightly cook the meat, surimi and pepper.

3 Allow the antipasti to drain, cut into small pieces and add together with the pesto. Season it all with the salt and pepper.

4 Divide up the filling between the tortillas. Roll them all up, fasten with cocktail sticks and sprinkle with cheese. Bake them all in the oven on the middle shelf for about 15 minutes.

TIP
If you would like to pep it all up then just dice a small chilli finely and stir it into the pesto.

Papusas

Preparation Time: approx. 1 hour

912 kcal/3832 kJ

Serves 4

450 g/1 lb plain flour
125 ml/4 ½ fl oz sparkling water
125 ml/4 ½ fl oz malt beer
salt
pepper
ground cardamom, clove and allspice
800 g/1 lb 12 oz of pheasant breast
200 g/7 oz of bacon
1 onion
200 g/7 oz of chanterelle mushrooms
1 Tbsp chopped thyme
1 Tbsp chopped rosemary
3 Tbsp orange marmalade
4 Tbsp of orange liqueur
4 Tbsp of pepper butter

1 Mix the flour together with the sparkling water, malt beer, salt, pepper, ground cardamom, clove and allspice into a smooth dough and allow to rest for 10 minutes.

2 Wash and dry the meat and the bacon and cut into small pieces. Peel the onion and dice. Clean and wash the chanterelles and cut into pieces.

3 Put the meat, bacon, onion and chanterelles through the coarse disc of the mincer. Then work in herbs, marmalade and liqueur. Season it all with salt, pepper, ground cardamom, clove and allspice.

4 Heat the pepper butter and fry the mixture in it for 6 minutes. Pre-heat the oven to 180 °C/355 °F/gas mark 4.

5 Roll out the dough on a floured surface and cut out 8 circles with a diameter of about 10 cm/4 in each.

6 Divide the filling up between the circles and fold the dough in half over the filling. Seal and decorate the edges with a fork. Prick the tops several times with a fork.

7 Place the papusas in the oven on the middle shelf and bake for about 16 minutes. Serve immediately.

Stir dough ingredients.

Cut out 8 circles.

Place the filling on them.

Seal and decorate the edges.

Paper Parcels

Preparation Time: approx. 1 hour
(plus time to marinate)

432 kcal/1814 kJ

Serves 4

800 g/1 lb 12 oz duck breast fillet
1 Tbsp lemon pepper
3 red onions
300 ml/10 ½ fl oz red wine
3 Tbsp raspberry vinegar
2 bay leaves, 6 cloves
2 sprigs of thyme
2 sprigs of rosemary
6 Tbsp walnut oil
100 g/3 ½ oz of risotto rice
1 l/1 pint 15 fl oz of vegetable stock
250 ml/9 fl oz mushroom stock
350 g/12 oz of frozen mixed vegetables
2 Tbsp butter
8 large sheets of baking paper

1 Wash and dry the meat and cut into thin slices. Put into a shallow dish.

2 Dust with lemon pepper. Peel onions, dice and mix with the red wine, raspberry vinegar, bay leaves, cloves, the leaves stripped from the sprigs of herbs and oil. Pour over the meat and allow to stand for about 1 hour.

3 Pre-heat the oven to 200 °C/ 390 °F/gas mark 6. Cook the rice in the stock according to the instructions on the packet. Then allow the vegetables to stand in the cooking liquid that remains for about 5 minutes. Then pour off the liquid and allow to drain.

4 Brown the meat in the butter for about 3 minutes on both sides. Lay out the sheets of baking paper on a work surface. Divide rice and vegetables between the sheets and cover with the duck breast. Fold into small parcels and bake on the middle shelf in the oven for about 12 minutes.

Quail Nests

Preparation Time: approx. 1 hour and 15 minutes

385 kcal/1617 kJ

Serves 4

200 g/7 oz frozen strudel pastry
8 quail
2 1/3 pints 12 fl oz poultry stock
½ bunch of lemon balm
40 ml/1 ½ fl oz herb liqueur
2 green peppers
2 red chillis
4 sticks of celery
4 onions
4 cloves of garlic
4 Tbsp chilli oil
6 Tbsp tomato puree
2 Tbsp paprika paste
salt, pepper
1 bunch of parsley

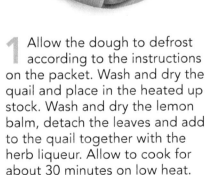

1 Allow the dough to defrost according to the instructions on the packet. Wash and dry the quail and place in the heated up stock. Wash and dry the lemon balm, detach the leaves and add to the quail together with the herb liqueur. Allow to cook for about 30 minutes on low heat.

2 In the meantime wash and dry the peppers, halve, core and then dice them.

3 Wash the chillis, halve and core them and then cut into strips. Clean and wash the sticks of celery and cut into pieces.

4 Peel the onions and dice. Peel the cloves of garlic and put through the garlic press. Heat the oil in a frying pan and lightly cook the peppers, chillis, celery, onions and garlic in it.

5 Add the tomato puree and the paprika paste and season it all to taste with salt and pepper. Wash and dry the parsley, cut into strips and likewise add.

6 Take the quail out of the stock, allow to drain and then separate the meat from the bone. Add to the vegetables. Pre-heat the oven to 180 °C/355 °F/gas mark 4. Place 2 sheets of strudel pastry on top of each other each time and cut into 4. Line 8 ovenproof pudding dishes with the double layer of pastry as shown above and pull the edges up such that they rise a little above the dishes.

7 Distribute the mixture between the dishes, placing it onto the pastry and push the edges lightly over it. Bake the pastry dishes in the oven on the middle shelf for about 20 minutes. Serve either warm or cold.

Sushi

Preparation Time: approx. 35 minutes

233 kcal/978 kJ

Serves 4

3 Nori leaves
400 g/14 oz ready-made sushi rice
wasabi paste to brush on
300 g/10 ½ oz smoked duck breast
1 avocado
lemon juice
4 Tbsp sweet and sour sauce

1 Dry roast the Nori leaves in a frying pan, lay onto a work surface and with a sharp knife cut each one into 6 equally large strips. Press the rice into 18 small balls with an elongated shape. Carefully wrap each Nori leaf round one of the rice balls. Stick the end of the Nori leaf to fasten with some wasabi paste or some rice kernels.

2 Brush the rice with some wasabi paste. Dice the duck breast. Halve the avocado, re-move the stone, peel the two halves, cut the flesh into small cubes and drizzle with lemon juice. Stir both up with the sauce and place onto the rice. Garnish according to taste.

Variation

Alternatively, fill the leaves with strips of turkey breast, capers, some soy sauce and finely chopped pieces of omelette.

Cut the Nori leaves.

Wind the strip round the rice.

Stick together using rice.

Brush the rice with wasabi paste.

Place the filling on top.

Prepared with Style: Fish and Seafood

Small parcels for great gourmets – from sushi to wan-tan, from pitta to strudel. You probably haven't met seafood in this form before! Ingredients from sea, lake and river are really clever space packers and completely versatile to prepare. Enjoy Neptune's favourite fishes, fine lobster vol au vents or deliciously-filled vine leaves!

Small Trout Strudels

Preparation Time: approx. 55 minutes

701 kcal/2944 kJ

Serves 4

200 g/7 oz frozen strudel pastry
3 strands of leak
2 fennel bulbs
1 bunch of spring onions
1 red chilli
1 red pepper
400 g/14 oz white turnips
4 Tbsp walnut oil
1 bunch each of dill and parsley
125 ml/4 ½ fl oz vegetable stock
salt, pepper
garlic powder
800 g/1lb 12 oz trout fillets
1 Tbsp lemon juice
2 Tbsp clarified butter
mayonnaise dip to serve

1 Defrost the pastry according to the instructions on the packet and spread out on a work surface. Clean and wash the leak and cut into rings.

2 Clean and wash the fennel and cut into strips. Clean and wash the spring onions and cut into rings. Clean and wash the chilli and cut into strips. Wash the pepper, halve lengthwise, core and cut into small pieces. Wash the turnips, peel and cut into strips.

3 Heat the oil in a frying pan and lightly cook the vegetables in it. Wash and dry the herbs, chop finely and add. After about 3 minutes, add the vegetable stock and allow to cook for about 4 minutes. Season with salt, pepper and garlic powder.

4 Wash and dry the fish fillets and drizzle with lemon juice.

5 Heat the clarified butter in a frying pan and fry the fish on both sides for about 4 minutes in it. Then cut into 8 pieces.

6 Pre-heat the oven to 180 °C/ 355 °F/gas mark 4. Cut the strudel pastry into 8 rectangles. Arrange portions of the vegetables on them.

7 Lay a piece of fish onto each one. Fold the edges in and fold the corners of the pastry over it. Bake the strudel pastries in the oven on the middle shelf for about 15 minutes.

8 Arrange the strudel parcels with a mayonnaise dip and serve.

Colourful Sturgeon Rolls

Preparation Time: approx. 40 minutes

552 kcal/2318 kJ

Serves 4

8 Chinese leaf leaves, salt
800 g/1 lb 12 oz of sturgeon fillet
400 g/14 oz of pickled beetroot
200 g/7 oz gherkins pickled with mustard
100 g/3 ½ oz of tinned sweet potatoes
1 red onion
4 Tbsp clarified butter
3 Tbsp fish stock, 20 ml/4 tsp vodka
½ tsp each of ground coriander, cumin and mustard powder
cornflour to thicken
200 g/7 oz keta caviar
200 g/7 oz crème fraîche
20 ml/4 tsp of aniseed schnapps
2 Tbsp herb butter
pumpernickel to serve

1 Wash the Chinese leaf leaves and blanch in lightly salted water for 2 minutes. Take out, drain and halve lengthwise. Wash and dry the fish filets and chop finely. Allow the vegetables to drain in a sieve and cut into pieces. Peel the onion and dice. Heat the clarified butter in a frying pan and lightly cook the fish in it. Add the vegetables and pour on the stock and the vodka. Season with salt, ground coriander, cumin and mustard powder. Thicken with cornflour. Allow to cook for a further 3 minutes.

2 Add the caviar to the crème fraîche and season to taste with aniseed schnaps, salt and mustard powder. Distribute the sturgeon and vegetable mixture onto the leaves. Fold the sides in and roll up. Fasten with a cocktail stick. Heat up the herb butter and brown the rolls in it for 3 minutes. Serve with pumpernickel and caviar cream.

TIP
If you can't manage to get any sturgeon then you can equally well use any fresh or frozen white fish.

111

Tomatillo Salsa

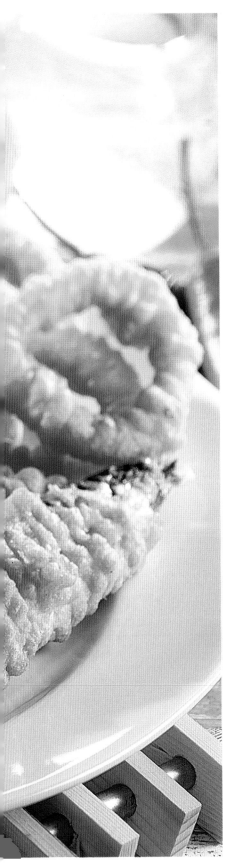

Preparation Time: approx. 45 minutes

677 kcal/2843 kJ

Serves 4

12 small frozen squid
12 scallops from jar
12 frozen tiger prawns
12 frozen sardines
3 Tbsp lemon juice, 4 egg yolks
500 ml/18 fl oz sparkling water
250 ml/9 fl oz chilled white wine
300 g/10 ½ oz plain flour
8 tomatillos
750 ml/1 pint 7 fl oz vegetable stock
4 cloves of garlic
½ bunch of coriander
1 red and 1 green chilli
flour for coating
oil for deep frying

1 Allow the seafood to defrost according to the instructions on the packets. Then drizzle with lemon juice. Mix the egg yolk together with the sparkling water, white wine and flour into a smooth batter. Allow to stand for 10 minutes.

2 Wash and dry the tomatillos and remove the skin. Heat the stock and allow the tomatillos to cook in it for about 6 minutes. Take out, allow to cool and dice. Peel the cloves of garlic and put through a garlic press. Wash and dry the coriander and detach the leaves.

3 Wash the chillis, halve lengthwise, core and cut into strips. Place the tomatillos, garlic, coriander and chillis in a pan and drizzle 8 Tbsps of the stock over them and allow to reduce somewhat. Coat the seafood in the flour, dip into the batter and then deep fry in hot oil. Serve the warm salsa with it.

Mix batter ingredients.

Coat the seafood in the flour.

Dip it all into the batter.

Deep fry until golden brown.

Shrimp Rolls

Preparation Time: approx. 45 minutes

435 kcal/1827 kJ

Serves 4

24 small frozen spring roll pastry sheets measuring 12.5 cm x 12.5 cm/5 x 5 in

500 g/1 lb 2 oz cooked, shelled prawns

200 g/7 oz tinned water chestnuts

½ bunch of spring onions

1 red chilli

1 Tbsp chopped ginger

2 Tbsp chopped lemongrass

salt

pepper

ground coriander and cumin

2 Tbsp light soy sauce

1 Tbsp fish sauce

oil for deep frying

1 Allow the sheets of pastry to defrost according to the instructions on the packet. Wash and dry the prawns, chop finely. Allow the chestnuts to drain in a sieve and likewise chop finely.

2 Clean and wash the spring onions and cut into thin rings. Wash the chilli and cut in half, core and cut into strips. Mix the prawns with chestnuts, spring onions, chilli, ginger and lemongrass. Season with salt, pepper, ground coriander and cumin, soy sauce and fish sauce.

3 Lay the pastry sheets out on a work surface and distribute the filling between them. Fold the sides over and roll it all up exerting a light pressure. Heat the oil in a deep fat fryer and fry the small rolls in it until golden brown.

Tuna Fish Pooris

Preparation Time: approx. 40 minutes

532 kcal/2236 kJ

Serves 4

100 g/3 ½ oz wholemeal flour
100 g/3 ½ oz plain flour
salt
ground coriander
500 ml/18 fl oz lukewarm water
5 Tbsp wheat beer
3 Tbsp butter
2 cloves of garlic
3 red onions
50 g/1 ¾ oz peeled tomatoes
2 Tbsp ready-made basil pesto
100 g/3 ½ oz pitted black olives
250 g/9 oz tinned tuna
2 Tbsp olive oil
pepper
2 Tbsp lemon juice
2 Tbsp clarified butter

3 Allow the olives to drain, chop finely and add. Allow the tuna fish to drain, separate roughly and mix in with the tomato mixture.

4 Stir in the oil and season everything to taste with salt, pepper and lemon juice.

5 Shape the dough into a roll on a lightly floured work surface and divide into portions. Press the pieces into flat rounds with a diameter of about 8 cm/ 3 ½ in each.

1 Work the flour together with the salt, ground coriander, water, wheat beer and butter into a smooth dough. Peel the garlic cloves and chop finely.

2 Peel the onions and dice. Squash the tomatoes with the back of a fork and mix together with the garlic, onion and pesto.

6 Place a portion of the filling onto one round and cover with a second. Seal the edges with a fork. Heat the clarified butter in frying pan and fry the pies in it for about 6 minutes on each side. Serve either warm or cold.

Lobster Pie

Preparation Time: approx. 1 hour and 30 minutes

947 kcal/3979 kJ

Serves 4

350 g/12 oz of plain flour, 1 tsp salt
150 g/5 oz of truffle butter
150 ml/5 fl oz lukewarm water
12 leaves of white gelatine
250 ml/9 fl oz light grape juice
250 ml/9 fl oz white wine
250 ml/9 fl oz lobster stock
1 Tbsp raspberry vinegar
1 pinch sugar
600 g/1 lb 5 oz tinned lobster
4 shallots, 1 red chilli
200 g/7 oz button mushrooms
1 bread roll from the previous day
1 bunch of chervil
2 Tbsp butter, 2 Tbsp sherry
1 tsp mustard
pepper
paprika
3 Tbsp double cream
butter for greasing the loaf tin
egg yolk and milk for brushing

Variation

Place the mixture into ready-made vol au vent cases, decorate and serve with the wine jelly cubes, which, if you like, can be further enhanced with chopped tarragon.

1 Work the flour together with the salt, truffle butter and water into a smooth dough and chill for about 10 minutes.

2 Soak the gelatine in cold water and press out. Place the juice, white wine, lobster stock, vinegar and sugar into a pan and heat up. Add the gelatine and dissolve it. Place all of this into a rectangular mould and allow to set in the refrigerator.

3 Dice the lobster. Peel the shallots and dice. Wash the chilli and cut in half lengthwise, core and chop finely. Clean and wash the button mushrooms and likewise dice. Grate the bread roll. Clean and wash the chervil, detach the leaves and chop finely.

4 Heat the clarified butter in a frying pan and lightly cook the lobster, shallots, chilli and mushrooms. Add the grated bread and the chervil. Use sherry to add aroma to it all. Season with mustard, salt, pepper and paprika. Stir in the double cream

5 Heat the oven to 200 °C/ 390 °F/gas mark 6. Take a medium size (2 lb) loaf tin and grease with butter. Roll out the dough and line the tin with it, allowing an edge to clear the tin all the way round.

6 Place the mixture into the tin and fold the pastry over it. Prick several times with a fork. Beat milk and egg yolk together in a bowl and brush the top of the pie with it and bake in the oven on the middle shelf for about 30 minutes.

7 Tip the jelly out of the mould and cut into cubes. Cut the pie into slices and serve with the wine jelly cubes.

Roll the pastry out.

Place the pastry into the loaf tin.

Fold the pastry over the filling.

Prick the pastry several times.

Filled Fish Sticks

Preparation Time: approx. 55 minutes
(plus time to marinate)

575 kcal/2415 kJ

Serves 4

750 g/1 lb 11 oz of plaice fillets
5 Tbsp herb vinegar
9 Tbsp olive oil
2 tsp herb mustard
3 red onions
1 Tbsp chopped garlic chives
salt
pepper
400 g/14 oz (frozen) seafood
1 yellow pepper
1 bunch of spring onions
3 tomatoes
½ bunch each of mint and parsley
cornflour to dust
3 Tbsp sunflower seed oil
1 cucumber

1 Wash and dry the fish fillets and lay in a shallow dish. Beat the vinegar, olive oil and mustard together.

2 Peel the onions and dice. Add the onions and garlic chives and season it all with salt and pepper. Drizzle the marinade over the fish and allow to stand for about 1 hour.

3 Defrost the seafood according to the instructions on the packet and chop finely. Wash the pepper, halve it, core and dice.

4 Clean and wash the spring onions and cut into thin rings. Wash the tomatoes and dice.

5 Wash and dry the herbs and chop finely. Drain the fish fillets. Mix the seafood with the paprika, spring onions, tomatoes and herbs and place the mixture on top of the fish fillets. Roll them all up and fasten with cocktail sticks. Dust with cornflour.

6 Heat the oil in a frying pan and fry the fish in it on all sides for about 6 minutes. Meanwhile wash the cucumber and cut into thick slices. Arrange the fish rolls on top of the cucumber slices and serve.

Hot Chalupas

Preparation Time: approx. 45 minutes

583 kcal/2448 kJ

Serves 4

2 Tbsp butter
8 medium sized ready-made tortillas
2 red peppers
2 yellow peppers
4 red onions
4 cloves of garlic
800 g/1 lb 12 oz of carp fillet
salt, pepper, paprika
4 Tbsp clarified butter
4 Tbsp red wine
200 g/7 oz tinned chilli beans
1 bunch of parsley
Rocket leaves to decorate

1 Heat the butter in a frying pan and fry the tortillas in it on both sides until golden brown. Fold in the middle and form a kind of ship so that the corners lie on top of each other and the middle is pushed out with the sides a distance from each other in the middle. Allow the tortillas to cool.

2 Wash and halve the peppers, core and cut into strips. Peel the onions and dice. Peel the cloves of garlic and chop finely. Wash and dry the carp fillets and dice. Season with salt, pepper and paprika. Heat the clarified butter in a frying pan and lightly cook the fish in it. Add the paprika, onions and garlic. Season with salt, pepper and paprika.

3 Add the red wine and allow to cook for 5 minutes. Allow the beans to drain in a sieve. Wash and dry the parsley, chop finely and add with the beans to the frying pan with the fish and vegetables. Allow to cook for about 4 minutes. Line the chalupas with the rocket leaves, put the filling in and serve up.

TIP
If you like, serve the chalupas with a fromage frais dip made with fresh herbs and garlic, seasoned to taste with salt and chilli powder.

Confetti Sardine Snails

Preparation Time: approx. 1 hour and 5 minutes

961 kcal/4788 kJ

Serves 4

350 g/12 oz plain flour	
250 g/9 oz low fat fromage frais	
150 g/5 oz chilled butter	
150 g/5 oz chilled roast onion butter	
salt	
150 g/5 oz frozen sardines	
2 Tbsp lemon juice	
4 Tbsp olive oil	
pepper	
450 g/1 lb frozen vegetable selection for frying	
100 g/3 ½ oz frozen herbes de Provence	
2 egg yolks	

1 Knead the flour with the fromage frais, butter and salt into a smooth dough. Roll out onto a floured work surface. Fold up and roll out. Repeat this several times. The more you do so, the lighter will be the puff pastry.

2 Allow the sardines to defrost as per instructions on the packet and drizzle with lemon juice. Heat the oil in a frying pan and fry the sardines in it on both sides for about 6 minutes each. Season with salt and pepper.

3 Prepare the vegetable selection for frying according to the instructions on the packet and add the defrosted herbs. Then purée with the hand-held blender. Spread the vegetables on the prepared pastry and lay sardines at the top of the pastry. Roll up from that side and cut into 2 cm/1 in wide discs.

4 Brush them all with the egg yolk and bake in the oven on the middle shelf for about 15 minutes until golden brown. Serve warm immediately.

Fold up the puff pastry.

Spread everything on the pastry.

Roll up the pastry.

Cut into discs.

Mackerel Bites

Preparation Time: approx. 45 minutes

677 kcal/2845 kJ

Serves 4

200 g/7 oz frozen strudel pastry
450 g/1 lb smoked mackerel fillets with pepper
¼ bunch of parsley
¼ bunch of chervil
¼ bunch of tarragon
¼ bunch of lemon thyme
3 Tbsp dry vermouth
4 Tbsp crème fraîche
salt
lemon pepper
150 g/5 oz fjord mussels from a jar

1 Allow the pastry to defrost according to the instructions on the packet. Cut every sheet of pastry into 4 parts and lay out on a work surface.

2 Cut the mackerel fillets into pieces. Wash and dry the herbs and chop finely. Mix with the vermouth and purée them all with the hand-held blender. Stir in the crème fraîche and season it all to taste with salt and lemon pepper.

3 Pre-heat the oven to 180 °C/ 355 °F/gas mark 4. Allow the mussels to drain in a sieve and then add to the herbs together with the pieces of mackerel.

4 Spread the mixture onto the pieces of pastry. Lay two pieces of pastry which have been thus spread on top of each other and twist together to look like a wrapped sweet.

5 Bake them all in the oven on the middle shelf for about 15 minutes.

California Sushi

Preparation Time: approx. 55 minutes

775 kcal/3255 kJ

Serves 4

8 Nori leaves
100 g/3 ½ oz 5 minute rice
1 tsp wasabi paste
3 Tbsp soy sauce, 4 Tbsp rice wine
450 g/1 lb of tinned crab meat
2 avocados
½ cucumber
½ bunch of spring onions
1 red chilli
3 Tbsp preserved ginger
3 Tbsp mayonnaise
2 Tbsp Chinese five spice
6 eggs
80 ml/2 ¾ fl oz sparkling water
salt
3 Tbsp butter

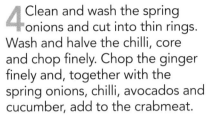

4 Clean and wash the spring onions and cut into thin rings. Wash and halve the chilli, core and chop finely. Chop the ginger finely and, together with the spring onions, chilli, avocados and cucumber, add to the crabmeat.

5 Drain the rice and likewise add to the mixture, mixing well. Stir the Chinese five spice into the mayonnaise and mix this into the rice mixture.

1 Dry roast the nori leaves in a frying pan without fat and then cut them in half lengthwise. Prepare the rice according to the instructions on the packet.

2 Mix the wasabi paste with the soy sauce and rice wine. Allow the crab meat to drain, squash with a fork and add to the sauce.

3 Wash the avocados, halve, remove the stone, peel the halves and dice finely. Wash the cucumber and dice finely.

6 Beat the eggs in a bowl, add the sparkling water and some salt. Heat the butter in a frying pan and cook thin omelettes out of the batter. Then cut into strips.

7 Divide the filling up and place onto the Nori leaves and roll up. Wrap a strip of omelette around each roll and stick the ends together with a grain of rice. Then serve.

Vineleaves

Preparation Time: approx. 35 minutes
(plus chilling time)

732 kcal/3076 kJ

Serves 4

36 preserved vine leaves
300 g/10 ½ oz smoked salmon
1 red chilli
3 Tbsp horseradish sauce
2 Tbsp curry powder
600 g/1 lb 5 oz cream cheese
lemon pepper
300 g/10 ½ oz herring fillets in paprika sauce
3 Tbsp coloured pickled peppers
1 green chilli
salt
paprika

1 Rinse the vine leaves well and soak in ice water for a short time. Then spread out onto a work surface and remove the base of the stalk. Chop the salmon finely.

2 Wash the red chilli, halve lengthwise, core and dice. Then mix with the salmon, horseradish sauce, curry powder and half of the cream cheese. Season to taste with lemon pepper.

3 Chop the herring fillets finely. Allow the pickled peppers to drain in a sieve and chop into small pieces.

4 Wash the green chilli, halve lengthwise, core and dice. Mix the herring fillets, paprika and chilli with the rest of the cream cheese. Season to taste with salt and paprika.

5 Spread half of the vine leaves with the salmon/cheese mixture and the other half with the herring/cheese mixture.

6 Fold the sides in and roll up the leaves. Chill them all for about 1 hour and serve.

Variation

This also works very well as a filling for the vine leaves tinned sardines mixed with cream cheese, a little basil pesto and pickled onions.

Remove the base of the stalk.

Mix the salmon and cheese.

Dice the chillis.

Mix the herring and vegetables.

Roll up the vine leaves.

125

Herring Piroggis

Preparation Time: approx. 50 minutes

1195 kcal/5019 kJ

Serves 4

150 g/5 oz of buckwheat flour
150 g/5 oz rye flour
1 tsp salt
150 g/5 oz cold butter
6 Tbsp wheat beer
5 shallots
250 g/9 oz beetroot from a jar
200 g/7 oz gherkins pickled with mustard
2 apples
2 Tbsp clarified butter
pepper
750 g/1 lb 11 oz herring fillets
1 bunch of dill
100 g/3 ½ oz cream cheese
milk for brushing
sunflower seeds to decorate

1 Work the flour, salt, butter and wheat beer into a pliable dough. Then allow to stand for about 10 minutes. Peel the shallots and dice.

2 Allow the beetroot and the gherkins to drain in a sieve and likewise dice. Peel the apples, halve, core and dice.

3 Heat the clarified butter in a frying pan and lightly cook the shallots, beetroot, gherkins and apples in it. Season with salt and pepper. Wash and dry the herring fillets and dice.

4 Wash and dry the dill, chop finely and add to the vegetables with fish and cream cheese. Allow to cook for about 4 minutes. Remove from the heat.

5 Pre-heat the oven to 180 °C/ 355 °F/gas mark 4. Roll the dough out onto a floured work surface and cut squares of 12 x 12 cm/5 x 5 in out.

6 Place portions of the filling onto the middle of each square and fold the pastry diagonally over the filling.

7 Press the sides together well. Brush the piroggis with milk and sprinkle the sunflower seeds over them. Bake the piroggis on the middle shelf in the oven for about 20 minutes.

Stuffed Pasta Mussel Shells

Preparation Time: approx. 45 minutes

647 kcal/2719 kJ

Serves 4

24 large pasta mussel shells

500 ml/18 fl oz lobster stock

500 ml/18 fl oz vegetable stock

3 Tbsp olive oil

salt

400 g/14 oz frozen mixed vegetables

3 Tbsp double cream

pepper

nutmeg

750 g/1 lb 11 oz of smoked halibut

½ bunch of lemon balm

½ bunch of parsley

100 g/3 ½ oz pitted black olives

24 small radicchio leaves

1 Cook the pasta shells in the stock with oil and salt for about 12 minutes.

2 Prepare the vegetables according to the instructions on the packet, then allow to drain, chop finely and mix with the double cream.

3 Season to taste with the salt, pepper and nutmeg. Dice the fish finely.

4 Wash and dry the herbs and chop finely. Allow the olives to drain and also cut into small pieces.

5 Add them all to the vegetables and mix well. Carefully take the pasta shells out and fill with the mixture.

6 Wash the radicchio and cut into strips. Arrange into nests on a serving dish. Place 1-2 pasta shells onto each nest and serve.

TIP

The filled pasta shells taste very good cold. If you would like to serve them up warm, you should place them in a large shallow ovenproof dish which has been greased with herb butter and sprinkle some grated cheese over them before placing in the oven.

Dutch Eel Rings

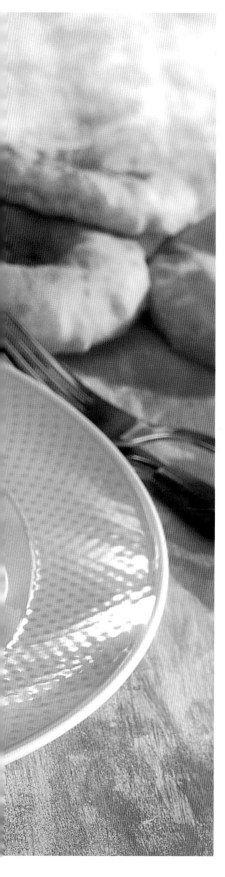

Preparation Time: approx. 45 minutes

1192 kcal/5008 kJ

Serves 4

300 g/10 ½ oz plain flour	
3 Tbsp crème fraîche	
300 ml/10 ½ fl oz water	
salt	
ground coriander	
800 g/1 lb 12 oz skinned smoked eel fillets	
200 g/7 oz bean sprouts	
150 g/5 oz cream cheese	
4 Tbsp bottled horseradish	
2 Tbsp lemon juice	
40 ml/1 ½ fl oz gin	
2 Tbsp capers	
pepper	
2 Tbsp clarified butter	

1 Work the flour together with the crème fraîche, water, salt and ground coriander into a smooth dough. Allow to stand for 10 minutes.

2 Wash and dry the eel fillets and cut into pieces. Wash and dry the bean sprouts. Stir the cream cheese up with the horse radish, lemon juice and gin.

3 Allow the capers to drain and add with the eel and bean sprouts to the cream cheese mixture. Purée it all with the hand-held blender such that a firm consistency arises. Season to taste with salt and pepper.

4 Roll the dough out onto a floured work surface and cut into 8 rectangles. Arrange portions of the filling along the long side of the rectangle and then roll it up from that side.

5 Shape the whole thing into a ring, flatten slightly and repeat. Heat clarified butter in a frying pan and fry the rings in the pan on both sides for about 6 minutes. Serve the rings with a cucumber salad.

Work everything into a dough.

Cut the pastry into rectangles.

Roll up and press flat.

Fry the rings.

Pittas with Fried Fish

Preparation Time: approx. 1 hour

408 kcal/1713 kJ

Serves 4

8 small pitta breads
8 small slices of plaice fillet
2 Tbsp lemon juice
2 eggs
salt
pepper
flour
4 Tbsp breadcrumbs for frying
2 Tbsp of grill butter (butter with tomato ketchup, parsley and a shallot)
200 g/7 oz bacon
300 g/10 ½ oz North Sea prawns
mayonnaise dip for serving

1 Briefly warm up the pittas in the oven and keep warm. Wash and dry the fish and drizzle with lemon juice.

2 Beat the eggs in a bowl and season with salt and pepper.

3 Dust the fish fillets with flour, dip into the egg and then coat with the breadcrumbs.

4 Heat the butter in a frying pan and then fry the fish fillets in it on both sides for about 6 minutes until golden brown.

5 Cut the bacon into strips and place in another frying pan without fat to melt off some of their fat.

6 Add the washed prawns and season with salt, pepper and a little lemon juice.

7 Place the fish into the pitas, add the bacon and the prawns and serve with a mayonnaise dip.

Fishballs

Preparation Time: approx. 50 minutes

910 kcal/3822 kJ

Serves 4

350 g/10 ½ oz plain flour
15 g/ ½ oz of dried yeast
salt
3 Tbsp olive oil
1 Tbsp baking powder
4 Tbsp white wine
200 ml/7 fl oz water
300 g/10 ½ oz frozen cockles
150 g/5 oz frozen shrimps
300 g/10 ½ oz frozen cod fillet
½ bunch of spring onions
1 red chilli
1 Tbsp chopped dill
1 Tbsp chopped parsley
2 Tbsp lemon juice
lemon pepper
garlic powder
3 Tbsp clarified butter

2 Allow the seafood to defrost according to instructions on the packet and cut into small pieces.

3 Clean and wash the spring onions and cut into thin rings. Wash and halve the chilli, core and chop finely. Mix together the seafood, spring onions, chilli, herbs and lemon juice and season with salt, lemon pepper and garlic powder.

1 Knead the flour together with the dried yeast, salt, olive oil, baking powder, white wine and water into a smooth dough. Then shape into about 32 small balls and allow to rest on a floured work surface for about 20 minutes.

4 Slightly squash the dough balls, pull apart and place the mixture into the hollow centres.

5 Press the balls together again. Heat clarified butter in a large pan and fry the balls all over for about 8 minutes.

Jellied Scallops

Preparation Time: approx. 50 minutes

195 kcal/819 kJ

Serves 4

100 g/3 ½ oz sea algae
8 leaves of white gelatine
250 ml/9 fl oz lobster stock
125 ml/4 ½ fl oz white wine
24 shelled scallops with roe
1 sachet of saffron
3 Tbsp pernod
½ bunch each of lemon balm and parsley
4 Tbsp pepper butter
100 g/3 ½ oz of frozen vegetables for soup
salt
pepper
tabasco

1 Line 8 small moulds with the sea algae. Soak the gelatine in cold water and press out. Heat the stock and the white wine in a pot and add the scallops, saffron and pernod.

2 Wash and dry the herbs, chop finely and add to the scallops. Allow to cook on low heat for about 4 minutes.

3 Then take the scallops out and allow to drain. Save the stock.

4 Heat the pepper butter in a frying pan and fry the scallops in it. Add the vegetables for soup and season well to taste with salt, pepper and tabasco.

5 Heat the stock and dissolve the gelatine in it. Take off the stove and use half the aspic to half fill the small moulds lined with sea algae.

6 Place the scallops on top of this and cover with the rest of the aspic. Allow to cool for about 1 hour in the refrigerator. Tip the jelly out of the small moulds onto plates and serve.

Variation

Arrange the scallops with the jelly in their own shells and serve.

Line the moulds with sea algae.

Partially fill the moulds with aspic.

Place the scallops in.

Cover with aspic.

Turn the jellies out.

Neptune's Favourite Fish

Preparation Time: approx. 1 hour and 20 minutes

782 kcal/3286 kJ

Serves 4

250 g/9 oz plain flour
250 g/9 oz herb butter
150 g/5 oz finely crumbled Nori leaf
salt
600 g/1 lb 5 oz frozen sea food
800 ml/1 pint 8 fl oz fish stock
8 Tbsp bulgar wheat
½ bunch of spring onions
¼ bunch each of mint and parsley
3 Tbsp tomato puree
1 Tbsp lemon juice
pepper
egg yolk for brushing

1 Knead the flour with the butter, Nori leaf and salt into a smooth dough and allow to rest for 10 minutes.

2 Defrost the sea food according to the instructions on the packet. Heat the stock in a pan and cook the sea food in it for about 8 minutes. Then allow to drain and cut into small pieces.

3 Stir the bulgar into the stock and allow it all to swell for 20 minutes. Pour away any excess liquid.

4 Clean and wash the spring onions and cut into thin rings. Wash and dry the herbs and chop finely.

5 Place the seafood together with the bulgar and the spring onions into a bowl and add the herbs, tomato purée and lemon juice. Season to taste with salt and pepper.

6 Pre-heat the oven to 180 °C/ 355 °F/gas mark 4. Roll the dough out onto a floured work surface and cut out 12 small fish shapes.

7 Place the filling into the middle of one fish shape and cover with another. Press the edges together and brush the top with egg yolk. Bake them all in the oven on the middle shelf for about 20 minutes.

"Espana" Tartlets

Preparation Time: approx. 45 minutes

502 kcal/2110 kJ

Serves 4

800 g/1 lb 12 oz anglerfish fillets
2 Tbsp lemon juice
2 aubergines
4 cloves of garlic
200 g/7 oz bottled pumpkin
4 Tbsp olive oil
4 Tbsp sherry
2 Tbsp chopped parsley
1 Tbsp chopped thyme
salt
pepper
allspice
paprika
16 ready-made savoury mini-tartlets

1 Wash and dry the fish, dice and drizzle the lemon juice over it.

2 Clean and wash the aubergines, dice.

3 Peel the cloves of garlic and chop finely. Allow the pumpkin to drain in a sieve and cut into small pieces.

4 Heat the oil in a frying pan and lightly cook the fish in it. Add the aubergines, garlic and pumpkin. Add sherry for aroma.

5 Add the herbs and season it all with salt, pepper, allspice and paprika.

6 Allow it all to cook for about 6 minutes on medium heat. Warm up the tartlets in the oven and put the filling into them. Serve them up lukewarm.

TIP
If you like you can put the filled tartlets into the oven with some grated Emmental cheese on them and heat until the cheese melts.

Wan-Tan Parcels

Preparation Time: approx. 55 minutes

218 kcal/916 kJ

Serves 4

500 g/1 lb 2 oz snapper fillets
1 l/1 ¾ pints fish stock
200 g/7 oz frozen vegetables for soup
2 Tbsp lemon juice
200 g/7 oz tinned chickpeas
1 large onion
1 Tbsp preserved ginger
200 g/7 oz tomato puree
4 Tbsp olive oil
salt
pepper
1 tsp each of ground cumin and paprika
6 egg whites
16 wan-tan sheets

1 Wash and dry the fish fillets and allow to cook for about 7 minutes in the hot stock together with the vegetables for soup.

2 Take out and allow to drain. Then cut into small pieces and drizzle with lemon juice.

3 Allow the chickpeas to drain in a sieve. Then lightly squash with the back of a fork and add to the fish.

4 Peel the onion and dice. Then cut the ginger into small pieces and brown with the onion and tomato puree in hot olive oil. Add to the fish and mix in thoroughly.

5 Season it all to taste with salt, pepper, ground cumin and paprika. Pre-heat the oven to 170 °C/340 °F/gas mark 3. Beat the egg white.

6 Cut the dough sheets in half, lay out on a work surface and brush with egg white. Place the fish and vegetable mixture in the middle of the pastry sheets.

7 Brush the corners of the dough sheets with egg white and fold over the filling to look like a parcel. Press lightly. Bake the parcels in the oven on the middle shelf for about 20 minutes.

Squash the chickpeas.

Brush the pastry sheets.

Place the filling on top.

Fold it all together.

Sweet Parcels: Desserts

Indulge yourself in sweet dreams and try our creamy through to fruity filled delicacies or crispy croissant, sometimes in fritters and sometimes as sweet pancakes. Not only as the ideal conclusion to any meal but also as a welcome change for in-between!

Cherry Papusas

Preparation Time: approx. 1 hour and 10 minutes

560 kcal/2352 kJ

Serves 4

450 g/1 lb plain flour
125 ml/4 ½ fl oz milk
125 ml/4 ½ fl oz sparkling water
1 tsp brown sugar
3 tsp vanilla sugar
450 g/1 lb sweet cherries
100 g/3 ½ oz brown sugar
125 ml/4 ½ fl oz cherry juice
250 ml/9 fl oz dry red wine
1 tsp ground cloves
3 cinnamon sticks
3 Tbsp cherry jam
2 Tbsp chopped almonds
1 Tbsp almond liqueur
possibly some cornflour, 1 egg

1 Mix a smooth dough from the flour, milk, sparkling water and vanilla sugar. Allow to rest for 10 minutes. Wash the cherries and stone them. Place the cherries, sugar, juice and red wine in a pan. Add the ground cloves and cinnamon sticks and allow it all to simmer for about 15 minutes.

2 Remove the cinnamon sticks and slightly squash the fruit with the back of a fork. Stir in the jam, almonds and almond liqueur. If necessary, stir in some cornflour which has already been stirred into a little water. Pre-heat the oven to 180 °C/355 °F/gas mark 4.

3 Roll the dough out onto a floured work surface and cut out circles with a diameter of about 7 cm/3 in. Distribute portions of the filling onto the circles. Fold over and seal the edges with a fork. Prick the upper surface of the papusas several times with a fork. Brush with egg. Bake them in the oven on the middle shelf for 15 minutes. Serve immediately.

Apples in Jackets

Preparation Time: approx. 1 hour

845 kcal/3549 kJ

Serves 4

150 g/5 oz plain flour
150 g/5 oz maize flour
100 g/3 ½ oz butter
½ tsp baking powder
1 egg, 1 egg yolk
50 g/1 ¾ oz brown sugar
1 tsp cinnamon
1 vanilla pod
8 small firm apples
2 Tbsp lemon juice
250 g/9 oz mascarpone cheese
3 Tbsp raisins
3 Tbsp chopped walnuts
125 ml/4 ½ fl oz apple juice
30 ml/1 fl oz apple schnapps
1 tsp ground cardamom
½ tsp ground cloves
egg yolk for brushing

3 Pre-heat the oven to 180 °C/ 355 °F/gas mark 4. Roll out the pastry thinly on a floured work surface and cut into 8 equally large squares.

4 Place the apples in the middle of the pastry squares and coat with the mascarpone mixture. Fold the corners of the pastry over the fruit and press down well.

5 Brush them all with the egg yolk. Then bake them all in the oven on the middle shelf for about 25 minutes. Custard goes well with these.

1 Work the flour with the butter, baking powder, egg, egg yolk, sugar and cinnamon into a smooth dough. Scratch out the innards of the vanilla pod and work into the dough and allow to rest for about 10 minutes.

2 Peel the apples, core using an apple corer and drizzle with lemon juice. Mix the mascarpone with the raisins, walnuts, apple juice, apple schnapps, ground cardamom and cloves.

Apricot Tarts

Preparation Time: approx. 1 hour and 25 minutes

767 kcal/3223 kJ

Serves 4

350 g/12 oz plain flour
½ tsp salt
150 g/5 oz butter
125 ml/4 ½ fl oz ice-cold water
1 kg/2 lb 3 oz apricots
6 Tbsp apricot liqueur
150 g/5 oz brown sugar
1 tsp each ground ginger, aniseed and cinnamon
2 Tbsp of small curls of butter milk chocolate coating to serve

1 Mix the flour with the salt, butter and ice-cold water into a smooth dough and allow to rest for about 10 minutes.

2 Wash the apricots, cut a cross into them and submerge briefly in boiling water. Dunk into the ice-cold water to cool, halve, stone and cut the flesh into strips.

3 Then drizzle with apricot liqueur, sprinkle with sugar and season with ground ginger, aniseed and cinnamon. Allow to stand for 20 minutes.

4 Pre-heat the oven to 180 °C/ 355 °F/gas mark 4. Roll the dough out on a floured work surface and cut circles with a diameter of about 6 cm/2 in each.

5 Distribute the apricot strips on them in such a way that there is a free edge all the way round. Pull these edges up and distribute the small curls of butter on them.

6 Press the edge somewhat over the filling. Brush the edges of the pastry with a little water.

7 Bake them all in the oven on the middle shelf for about 35 minutes. Pipe stripes of chocolate over them to serve.

Variation

Instead of the apricots, fresh blueberries or raspberries can be used. To give aroma use either herb schnapps or raspberry schnapps.

Cut into the apricots.

Submerge in hot water.

Skin the apricots.

Then halve.

Cut the halves into strips.

143

Kumquat Fritters

Preparation Time: approx. 50 minutes

422 kcal/1774 kJ

Serves 4

150 g/5 oz plain flour
1/2 tsp salt
200 ml/7 fl oz milk
8 Tbsp brown sugar
1/2 tsp each of ground cinnamon and coriander
1 vanilla pod, 2 eggs
750 g/1 lb 11 oz kumquats
125 ml/4 ½ fl oz white rum
125 ml/4 ½ fl oz brown rum
2 balls vanilla ice cream
8 Tbsp thick sweet creamed coconut
20 ml/4 tsp Batida de coco
4 Tbsp fromage frais
oil for deep frying

1 Work the flour, salt, milk, sugar, ground cinnamon and coriander into a smooth dough. Scrape the innards of the vanilla pod out and work into the batter.

2 Separate the eggs and add egg yolk to the batter. Beat the egg white until stiff and carefully fold in. Wash and dry the kumquats and prick several times with a fork or score several times with a knife but not too deeply.

3 Place them into a bowl and drizzle the rum over them. Allow to stand for 30 minutes.

4 To make the coconut cream: place the ice cream with the creamed coconut, liqueur and fromage frais into a bowl and stir until smooth. Chill thoroughly for about 20 minutes.

5 Allow the kumquats to drain, dry and dip into the batter.

6 Then deep fry in hot oil for about 5 minutes until golden brown. Use kitchen towel to absorb the excess oil and serve with the cold coconut cream.

Palmiers with Fruit

Preparation Time: approx. 50 minutes

590 kcal/2478 kJ

Serves 4

200 g/7 oz frozen puff pastry
flour to work it
650 g/1 lb 7 oz frozen mixed exotic fruit
250 g/9 oz cream cheese
2 Tbsp lemon juice
3 Tbsp grated lemon peel
4 Tbsp brown sugar
4 Tbsp ginger jam
1 bunch of mint
1 egg

1 Defrost the puff pastry according to the instructions on the packet and lay out on a floured work surface.

2 Mix the defrosted mixed fruit together with the cream cheese, lemon juice, lemon peel, sugar and ginger jam.

3 Wash and dry the mint, chop coarsely and add to the fruit mixture. Purée it all with the hand-held blender.

4 Pre-heat the oven to 180 °C/355 °F/gas mark 4. Roll out the dough into several rectangles which are not too thin. Spread the fruit mixture onto the sheets of pastry, leaving a small clear edge all the way round.

5 Roll in from both long edges at the same time towards the middle. Then cut the roll into 2 cm/1 in wide slices. Brush them all with egg.

6 Bake the palmiers in the oven on the middle shelf for about 18 minutes until golden brown.

TIP

If you like, spread the palmiers with melted dark chocolate coating before serving.

Tipsy Mango Crescents

Preparation Time: approx. 50 minutes

764 kcal/3208 kJ

Serves 4

250 g/9 oz plain flour
250 g/9 oz chilled butter
250 g/9 oz ground almonds
1/2 tsp sugar
orange peel essence
3 mangoes
4 Tbsp amaretto liqueur
1 tsp lemon juice
200 g/7 oz blackberries
3 Tbsp brown sugar
2 Tbsp maple syrup
flour for rolling out
2 egg yolks for brushing on

1 Work the flour together with the butter, almonds, sugar and orange peel essence into a smooth dough and allow to stand for about 15 minutes.

2 Wash and peel the mangoes, remove the stone and dice the flesh. Drizzle with amaretto and lemon juice and allow to stand for about 5 minutes.

3 Wash the blackberries and purée them with the hand-held blender and then add to the diced mangoes together with the sugar and maple syrup. Mix everything well.

4 Pre-heat the oven to 180 °C/ 355 °F/gas mark 4. Roll the dough out onto a floured work surface and cut into squares of 10 x 10 cm/4 x 4 in.

5 Divide the fruit mixture between them and roll the pastry squares up from one corner. Shape into crescents. Brush them all with egg yolk and bake in the oven on the middle shelf for about 18 minutes.

Dice the mangoes.

Purée the blackberries.

Divide the fruit.

Roll them all up.

Chocolate Strawberry Bites

Preparation Time: approx. 50 minutes

870 kcal/3654 kJ

Serves 4

16 sheets of filo pastry
750 g/1 lb 11 oz fresh strawberries
1 Tbsp brown sugar
½ tsp vanilla essence
2 Tbsp lemon juice
300 g/10 ½ oz cream cheese
6 Tbsp apple jelly
150 g/5 oz milk chocolate
150 g/5 oz melted butter

1 Pre-heat the oven to 180 °C/ 355 °F/gas mark 4. Lay the sheets of pastry between damp cloths. Wash the strawberries and cut in half, remove the stalks and cut the fruit into small pieces.

2 Mix up the pieces of fruit with sugar, vanilla essence and lemon juice. Stir in the cream cheese and apple jelly. Chop the chocolate finely and likewise stir into the mixture.

3 Lay the pastry sheets next to each other on a work surface and brush with the melted butter. Place another three sheets on top of each of four pastry sheets.

4 Cut circles out of the pastry slabs with a diameter of about 8 cm/3 in. Spread half of the circles with the cream cheese mixture and cover with the rest of the circles. Place the pastry layers on top of each other and press lightly.

5 Bake them all in the oven on the middle shelf for about 20 minutes. Serve warm.

Filled Pancakes

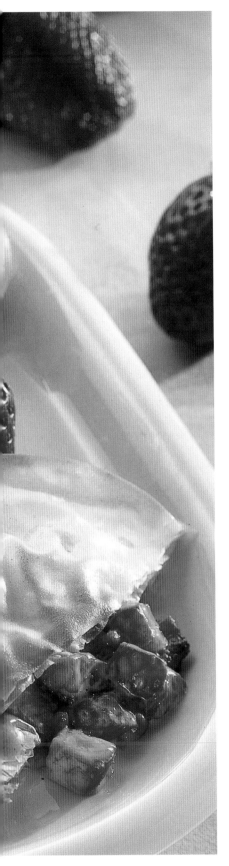

Preparation Time: approx. 40 minutes

675 kcal/2835 kJ

Serves 4

175 g/6 oz plain flour
1 pinch salt
6 tsp vanilla sugar
250 ml/9 fl oz milk
some sparkling water
3 eggs
100 g/3 ½ oz sultanas
150 g/5 oz walnuts
2 Tbsp lemon juice
1 Tbsp lemon peel essence
250 g/9 oz low fat fromage frais
3 Tbsp double cream
40 ml/1 ½ fl oz rum
4 Tbsp strawberry jam
ground cardamom and cinnamon
4 Tbsp butter
icing sugar for dusting

3 Mix the sultanas and nuts with the lemon juice, lemon peel essence, fromage frais, double cream, rum and strawberry jam. Season to taste with the ground cinnamon and cardamom.

4 Heat the butter in a frying pan and make 16 small thin pancakes out of the batter.

5 Take them out, divide filling between them and roll up. Dust immediately with icing sugar and serve.

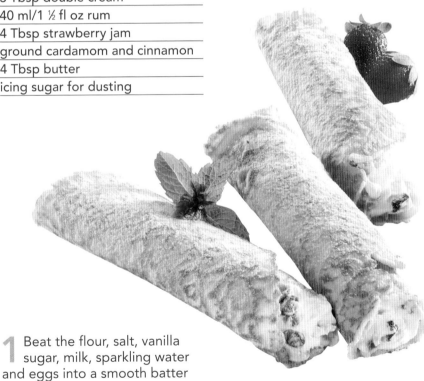

1 Beat the flour, salt, vanilla sugar, milk, sparkling water and eggs into a smooth batter and allow to rest for 10 minutes.

2 Wash and dry the sultanas and chop coarsely together with the nuts.

Sweet Spicy Eclairs

Preparation Time: approx. 1 hour

440 kcal/1848 kJ

Serves 4

200 ml/7 fl oz water
40 g/1 ½ oz butter
salt
ground cinnamon, ginger, cloves and custard powder
120 g/4 ¼ oz plain flour
1 pinch of baking powder
2 eggs
300 ml/10 ½ fl oz champagne
3 Tbsp brown sugar
1 Tbsp grated lemon peel
1 Tbsp lemon juice
ground cardamom
250 g/9 oz seedless green grapes
250 g/9 oz mandarins
150 g/5 oz mascarpone cheese

Variation

You can make any shape you wish from the choux pastry. Instead of the éclairs, for example, just pipe rings.

1 Bring water, butter, salt, ground cinnamon, ginger, cloves and custard powder to the boil. Sprinkle in flour and baking powder and stir until the dough separates from the bottom of the pan. Place it all into a bowl and knead the eggs into it. Allow to rest for 10 minutes.

2 Pre-heat the oven to 200 °C/ 390 °F/gas mark 6. Fill the dough into an icing bag and pipe bone-shapes onto a baking sheet.

3 Bake them all in the oven on the middle shelf for about 15 minutes until golden yellow. Cut the éclairs into halves whilst still warm, slightly hollow them out and allow to cool. In the meantime, prepare the filling.

4 Stir the champagne with sugar, salt, lemon peel, lemon juice and ground cardamom. Bring to the boil in a pan and allow to reduce to half in volume.

5 Wash the grapes, cut in half and add. Peel the mandarins to the pith, cut out the individual segments and cut into small pieces. Likewise add and allow flavours to develop for about 5 minutes on low heat.

6 Then allow to cool and stir in the mascarpone. Fill the éclairs with the mixture and serve.

Dough must separate from bottom.

Pipe dough into "bones".

Cut the éclairs in half.

Cut the grapes in half.

Fill the éclairs with the mixture.

Sweet Peanut Rolls

Preparation Time: approx. 50 minutes

1300 kcal/5460 kJ

Serves 4

200 g/7 oz plain flour
200 g/7 oz buckwheat flour
2 sachets of dried yeast
2 tsp brown sugar
150 g/5 oz soft butter
125 ml/4 ½ fl oz milk
3 Tbsp poppy seeds
100 g/3 ½ oz chopped candied lemon peel
2 Tbsp olive oil
100 g/3 ½ oz peanut butter
400 g/14 oz ground unsalted peanuts
200 g/7 oz unrolled oats
3 bananas
1 Tbsp honey
2 Tbsp lemon juice
1 tsp each of custard powder, ground cardamom and ginger
2 eggs
150 g/5 oz each of white and dark chocolate couverture

1 Work the flour with the yeast, sugar, butter, milk, poppy seeds and lemon peel into a smooth dough. Cover and allow to rise for 20 minutes.

2 Then shape a roll out of the dough and cut into 12 pieces. Place the peanut butter together with the peanuts and oats into a bowl and melt over a pan of simmering water.

3 Peel the bananas and cut into small pieces. Mix with honey, lemon juice, the custard powder and the ground cardamom and ginger.

4 Work the eggs into the mixture and fold into the peanut mixture. Pre-heat the oven to 180 °C/355 °F/gas mark 4. Shape small balls out of the dough.

5 Push in the middles of the balls somewhat and place a portion of the peanut mixture inside each one.

6 Then press back together and brush them all with the beaten eggs. Bake them all in the oven on the middle shelf for about 30 minutes.

7 Melt the chocolate and place in a small icing bag. Decorate alternate rolls by piping melted light and dark chocolate and serve.

Strawberry Rice Rolls

Preparation Time: approx. 45 minutes

310 kcal/1302 kJ

Serves 4

24 small sheets of rice pastry
100 g/3 ½ oz of cooked pudding rice
4 Tbsp sea buckthorn jelly
400 g/14 oz fresh strawberries
3 Tbsp cinnamon sugar
100 g/3 ½ oz of grated coconut
4 Tbsp of coconut cream
3 Tbsp clarified butter
vanilla ice cream to serve

1 Cut the rice pastry sheets in half and wrap up in damp tea towels. Cook the pudding rice through according to the instructions on the packet and fold in the sea buckthorn jelly.

2 Wash and dry the strawberries and cut into small pieces. Then mix with the cinnamon sugar, grated coconut and coconut cream.

3 Fold everything into the cooked pudding rice. Lay out half of the pastry sheets on a work surface and divide the rice and fruit mixture between them.

4 Cover with the pastry sheets left, fold in the sides and roll the sheets up. Heat the clarified butter in a frying pan and fry the rolls in it on all sides until golden brown. Serve the rice rolls with the vanilla ice cream.

TIP
The strawberry rolls are an ideal light fruity summer dish.

Baklava

Preparation Time: approx. 50 minutes

444 kcal/1864 kJ

Serves 4

8 filo pastry sheets
butter for greasing
250 ml/9 fl oz maple syrup
450 g/1 lb brown sugar
250 ml/9 fl oz water
1 Tbsp grated lemon peel
1 vanilla pod, 2 tsp ground cinnamon
400 g/14 oz walnuts
250 g/9 oz almonds
½ tsp each ground cardamom and cloves
200 g/7 oz melted butter

1 Lay the pastry sheets out on a work surface and wrap in damp tea towels. Grease a baking sheet with butter. Mix the maple syrup with 250 g/9 oz of the sugar, water, lemon peel, contents of the vanilla pod and 1 tsp of the ground cinnamon and bring to the boil. Allow to simmer on low heat for about 10 minutes. Then allow to cool slightly.

2 Pre-heat the oven to 180 °C/ 355 °F/gas mark 4. Grind the walnuts and almonds coarsely and mix with the rest of the sugar, cinnamon, cardamom and cloves. Spread out the pastry sheets and cut out 32 circles with a diameter of about 8 cm/3 in. Brush the circles with butter. Place 1 Tbsp of the filling onto each circle and drizzle syrup over them all.

3 Place four circles in all one over the other with the filling in between and then place them all onto the baking sheet. Then bake in the oven on the middle shelf for about 15 minutes.

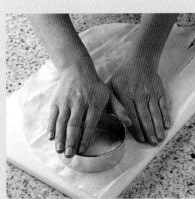

Cut circles out.

Brush with butter.

Put the mixture on top.

Drizzle with syrup.

Croissants with Mandarin Cream

Preparation Time: approx. 45 minutes

737 kcal/3097 kJ

Serves 4

400 g/14 oz frozen croissant pastry
250 g/9 oz cream cheese
5 Tbsp lemon marmalade
5 Tbsp orange marmalade
2 Tbsp each of lemon and orange juice
200 g/7 oz tinned mandarins
100 g/3 ½ oz icing sugar
a little lemon juice

1 Allow the pastry to defrost according to the instructions on the packet and cut each sheet diagonally so that triangles result. Pre-heat the oven to 180 °C/ 355 °F/gas mark 4.

2 Mix the cream cheese together with the marmalade and the juice. Allow the mandarins to drain in a sieve, keeping the juice. Cut the mandarins into small pieces and stir into the cream cheese.

3 Divide it all up onto the triangles and roll up the pastry from one corner into croissants. Curve the ends round. Bake them all in the oven on the middle shelf for about 20 minutes until golden brown.

4 Dissolve the icing sugar in the mandarin juice with a little lemon juice, place into an icing bag and use to decorate the croissants. Allow to dry and serve.

Fruit Pockets

Preparation Time: approx. 50 minutes

680 kcal/2856 kJ

Serves 4

150 g/5 oz plain wholemeal flour
200 g/7 oz plain flour
2 eggs
5 egg yolks
3 Tbsp multi vitamin juice
4 pears
250 g/9 oz blackberries
2 Tbsp lemon juice
100 g/3 ½ oz ground almonds
2 Tbsp brown sugar
1 tsp ground cinnamon
½ tsp each of ground cardamom and cloves
egg white for brushing on
salt
2 Tbsp butter

3 Wash and dry the blackberries and cut into small pieces. Drizzle lemon juice over both fruits.

4 Add the almonds, sugar, ground cinnamon, cardamom and cloves and mix well. Roll out the dough onto a floured work surface and cut into rectangles of about 6 x 8 cm/2 x 3 in.

5 Divide the filling up between them and leave a narrow edge. Brush the edges with egg white and fold the dough over.

1 Sieve the flour onto a work surface and make a well in the middle. Place the eggs, egg yolks and juice into the well and knead to make a smooth dough. Chill for about 10 minutes.

2 Peel the pears, quarter and remove the core. Cut into dice.

6 Press the edges together and cook the pockets in lightly salted water for about 8 minutes.

7 Take out and allow to drain. Heat the butter in a frying pan and fry the fruit pockets in it on both sides.

Puff Pastry Cones

Preparation Time: approx. 55 minutes

632 kcal/2654 kJ

Serves 4

250 g/9 oz plain flour
250 g/9 oz chilled butter
250 g/9 oz grated almonds
½ tsp sugar
orange peel essence
butter for greasing
3 egg yolks
200 g/7 oz mascarpone cheese
8 Tbsp brown sugar
4 Tbsp rose water
4 Tbsp each of orange and lemon juice
2 oranges
organic rose petals to garnish

Variation

Brew a strong fruit tea for the filling, season this to taste with ginger, cardamom and cinnamon and then stir into the cream cheese. Serve it all up garnished with lemon balm.

1 Work the flour together with the butter, almonds and orange peel essence into a smooth dough and allow to rest for about 15 minutes. Then roll out and cut into squares. Pre-heat the oven to 220 °C/430 °F/gas mark 7.

2 Cut aluminium foil squares to match and grease with butter. Shape the pieces of foil into cones, making sure that the greased side is on the outside.

3 Lay the puff pastry pieces around these and brush with egg yolk. Place the cones, with the side which overlaps the other on the underneath, on the middle shelf of the oven and bake for 18 minutes until golden brown.

4 Then carefully pull the foil out and allow the cones to cool on a cooling rack.

5 Mix the mascarpone with the sugar, rose water and juice. Peel the oranges so that the pith is removed. Separate the oranges into individual segments. Then cut the segments into pieces and mix into the cream cheese.

6 Fill the cones with the cream cheese mixture and serve garnished with the rose petals and sugar.

Shape the puff pastry into cones.

Peel the oranges.

Separate the segments.

Stir into the cream cheese.

Fill the cones with the mixture.

Recipe Index